Found

A MEMOIR

JENNIFER LAUCK
the true sequel to the *New York Times* bestseller *Blackbird*

SEAL PRESS

FOUND
A MEMOIR

Published by
Seal Press
A Member of the Perseus Books Group
1700 Fourth Street
Berkeley, California

Library of Congress Cataloging-in-Publication Data

Lauck, Jennifer.
  Found : a memoir / Jennifer Lauck.
    p. cm.
  ISBN 978-1-58005-367-9
  1. Lauck, Jennifer. 2. Adoptees—United States—Biography. 3. Abandoned children—United States—Biography. 4. Birthparents—United States. 5. Identity (Psychology) I. Title.
  HV874.82.L378 A3 2011
  362.734092—dc22
                    2010038734

Cover and interior design by Domini Dragoone
Cover painting and interior art © Blair Tyler Peters
Printed in the United States of America by RR Donnelley
Distributed by Publishers Group West

The author has changed some names, places, and recognizable details to protect the privacy of people mentioned in the book.

For Spencer & Josephine

My Beloveds

"In all of us there is a hunger, marrow-deep, to know our heritage—
to know who we are and where we have come from. Without this
enriching knowledge, there is a hollow yearning. No matter what
our attainments in life, there is still a vacuum, an emptiness,
and the most disquieting loneliness."

—Alex Haley

CONTENTS

AUTHOR COMMENT

Blackbird was a book I needed to write. Dead parents, a spate of homelessness, and countless moves from Nevada to California and back to Nevada had me emerge from my childhood in a spinning haze.

The voice I discovered was that of a child who seemed to be in shock. Writing was like debriefing a disoriented witness. As I wrote, I tried to form opinions about all I had gone through, but like my narrator, I could only feel numb and amazed. I found myself asking a series of questions instead: *Did my life have some meaning beyond all the loss? Was there some higher purpose to suffering? Could a person heal from such a childhood?*

Over the next few years, a series of extraordinary events unfolded and are detailed within this book. It seemed that in writing *Blackbird*, I had begun a long journey that, in the end, would provide answers to all my questions and much more.

Blackbird was a witness account conveyed by a little girl. *Found* is a widened perspective narrated by a reflective woman and mother. Both memoirs are my truth. As part of the creative process, I have taken liberty with conversations, with time, and with identity.

My great hope is that this story will be of benefit to all who read it.

—JENNIFER LAUCK

PORTLAND, OREGON

2010

"I am now seventy-one years old, I feel, still, deep in my mind, my first experience, my mother's care. I can still feel it. That immediately gives me inner peace, inner calmness. The mother's physical touch is the greatest factor for the healthy development of the brain. This is not due to religious faith, but because of the biological factor."

—His Holiness the Dalai Lama
Vancouver Dialogues
2007

"The separation from the mother's body, at birth, is the most dreadful thing. The baby was one with the mother and then the people take the child away and put him somewhere else. Dreadful."

—ECKHART TOLLE
FREEDOM FROM THE WORLD

ONE

WHEN I WAS BORN

I WAS GIVEN the perfect name, although it would take the better part of forty-six years to puzzle this perfection out.

Jennifer, popular in the '60s, is my first name and seems on the surface to be a fad. But in the end, it is my first name that leads me home.

Lauck, my last name, is the family surname and a German derivative of *lock*. *Lock* weaves a path of connection, at the root, to the verb form of *luck*. Coincidently, pull *a* from Lauck and there it is again. Luck. Of all the things I have been in this life, it is most accurate to say I've been lucky, indeed.

And here comes Caste, my middle name, which is core to the circumstances from which I began my life.

Caste originates from the Latin *castus*, meaning chaste, pure, innocent. As *caste* traveled through Portugal and Spain, it shifted to *casto*, meaning lineage, race, breed. In English, caste most often loses its silent *e* and becomes just *cast*.

While there are many meanings to the word *cast*, the markers on my map are these: to cast is to throw something away from yourself, usually with force; to cast also means to remove or banish something from your mind deliberately, decisively, and often with great difficulty. A castaway is one set adrift. An outcast has been rejected by a particular group or by society as a whole.

I WAS BORN in Nevada, which jigsaws against California. Most Nevadans occupy the narrow band of land situated along the western and southern borders. The population clusters in the big cities of Las Vegas, Carson City, and Reno, and then spreads wide in the smaller towns of Elko, Fallon, and Lovelock.

The largest part of Nevada is owned by the military and is unoccupied. At the bottom corner of the state, five hundred miles from Reno and seventy-five miles from Vegas, the U.S. Department of Energy operates the Nevada Test Site. Between 1951 and 1992, more than a thousand nuclear bombs were detonated at the Nevada Test Site. Octopus clouds could be seen from Las Vegas and it was not uncommon for tourists to gather on hotel balconies to gape at supernatural detonations that smeared the sky.

I wonder what these day-trippers thought as they watched tendrils of radioactive debris spiral back to earth. Were they afraid? Or did they feel proud, confident, and safe somehow, in the knowledge that these bombs were being perfected? And what of their senses? Did they notice the texture of the air transform from clear and clean to spiky and bright? Underfoot, did they feel the earth buck and then collapse? Could they detect any reorganization of atoms within their own cells?

OVER THE MONTHS I gestated, during 1963, more than forty nuclear bombs were detonated at the Nevada Test Site. They were given names like Chipmunk, Gerbil, and Pleasant. The combined explosive power of those blasts was equal to thirty-eight attacks on Hiroshima.

MY MOTHER WAS named Catherine. She lived in Reno and had blond hair and a heart-shaped face. Her eyes were a dove-soft shade of medium blue that might be called gray. She was seventeen.

My mother's boyfriend was Bill. He was also seventeen and had moved to Reno from California. Bill was a tall, awkward teen who passed time with the boys who wore leather jackets and smoked cigarettes from packs rolled in their sleeves.

Being unmarried, pregnant, and a teenager in 1963 was a dangerous combination that blew nuclear families wide open. Loyalties melted. Love vaporized. Protection was withdrawn. Shamed and afraid, the girls were scuttled to secret locations. Evidence of their pregnancies was hidden. Once babies were born, papers were signed, birth certificates were altered, and files were sealed.

Catherine had heard the whispers about girls who got pregnant and knew they always vanished from the halls and the classrooms of her high school. She didn't admit to being pregnant herself until she was five months along.

On a July morning, on or about the day a super bomb called The Sedan was dropped at the Nevada Test Site, Catherine told the truth.

In the same way the Nevada Test Site became a national sacrifice zone, meaning it became uninhabitable forevermore, Catherine's teen landscape evaporated. Gone were the simple times of drive-in movies, date nights, and long, languid kisses in the back seat of a souped-up Chevy while "Moon River" spilled from the radio. No more whispered secrets to her best friend on the telephone, no more "Dear Diary, I kissed a boy for the first time," and no more dreams of white weddings and picket fences waiting in the future.

Catherine's world became an unfamiliar and unforgiving place. She was humiliated by her family, isolated from friends, forbidden to see Bill again, and restricted to her bedroom for the duration of her pregnancy. The only person allowed near Catherine was a private tutor with the unusual name of Carmel. Her name was not pronounced like Carmel, the sea-splashed town below Monterey, California. Carmel came out of the mouth as *car-mull*, like one might refer to caramel apples or caramel corn.

Bill wanted to marry Catherine. He believed it was right for a child to have a name and a father. His own father had disappeared before he had been born. His mother wasn't even clear who his father had been—perhaps a man with the name Hamilton, or it could have been Wright. The vacuum in Bill's life was something he didn't want a child of his own to experience.

Catherine's family refused the marriage option. Catherine was considered irresponsible and immature. Bill was classified as trash and banished. Relinquishment was prearranged with Catholic Community Services of Northern Nevada.

OVER THAT LONG fall and into the winter, Catherine wept—of course she wept. She was scared, ashamed, and utterly alone. She kept up her schoolwork, though, and read a few novels to pass the time. Her favorite book was the Pulitzer Prize winner *Gone with the Wind*, that sweeping tale of the United States divided between north and south. The central character was Southern Belle Scarlett O'Hara and her home was the plantation Tara. Scarlet, spoiled and indulged, had to grow up during the Civil War and in the end, acquired strength from the land—from Tara.

Something in *Gone with the Wind* sparked inspiration in Catherine and she named me Tara and called me by that name again and again.

Did Catherine think, perhaps, if she named me then she would keep me? Or did she name me this so that I might become her strength? Or perhaps, like a good mother, she set this name into my heart as a way to give me the strength of the land, which I'd need if I didn't have a mother.

Through the power of my mother's imagination, she was able to transform me into something far greater than a dreadful mistake. And in naming me Tara, she also gave me directions home.

IN SEPTEMBER 1963, the Cuban and Russian governments placed nuclear bombs in Cuba.

In October 1963, the Cuban Missile Crisis ended when the Russian government agreed to dismantle the weapons in Cuba and the U.S. government agreed to dismantle similar nuclear weapons in Turkey.

In November 1963, John F. Kennedy was assassinated.

In December 1963, I was born to Catherine and taken away.

TWO

WHAT CANNOT BE SEEN

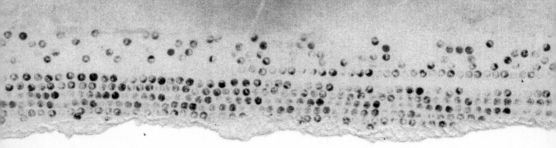

IT'S HARD TO FOCUS and seeing into the distance is impossible. My eyes work best when I squint and I squint a lot.

One of my first memories is linked to my poor vision. I have a deep sense of strain between my eyes. This tension has been with me all of my life.

THERE'S A LEGEND about Christopher Columbus. When his armada arrived in the new world, the native people could not see the ships. In all their lives and in the lives of their ancestors, no one had seen a ship before and so their brains did not have the experience needed to discern the shapes. A shaman came to the edge of the cliffs, looked at the ripples on the surface of the water, and noticed the current was unusual. After many days, the ships came into his view. The shaman told his people about the ships and eventually the people could see.

Is MY FIRST memory about sight? Or is my first memory actually the inability to recognize what was happening—or better stated, what wasn't happening?

It remains, all these years later, inconceivable that my mother wasn't the first person I saw.

If I would venture to guess at my first thought, I am sure it would have been this: *Where is she?*

WHEN I AM an adult, an optometrist will say I have the strangest muscles in my eyes. "You work very hard, as if you want to see what's not there."

I will need glasses by the time I am ten.

As a younger child, I will develop the quirk of studying each location where I live or travel. I'll take inventory of houses, neighborhoods, restaurants, office buildings, and churches. And I'll stare at the people I live with until someone inevitably says, "For heaven's sake, what are you looking at?"

By the time I am four or maybe five, I won't remember that my eyes search for my mother. Like dirt thrown into a deep hole, primal conditioning will be buried under the minutiae of details that become my life.

IT IS NOT a stretch of the imagination to say I searched for my mother from the moment I was born. A baby, indeed, searches for its mother—frantically so when the mother cannot be found.

Sight is the most used sense and the one most aligned with thought. More than eighty percent of what happens in the brain is related to sight. Yes, looking would come first. The thought *Where is she?* would certainly be one of the initial coherent thoughts.

I would have also listened, intently, for the timbre of her voice; I would have tested the air for her scent; I would have reached out to make contact; and I would have salivated in anticipation of her milk.

Babies are sensory creatures with highly developed brains.

What is not commonly known—although it is common sense—is that within moments of separation from the mother, a newborn will experience outrage, panic, and eventually terror. Within forty-five minutes, studies show a baby will go into shock and lose consciousness. Once the baby awakens, she will use her senses to search for her mother again and if the mother isn't there, the baby goes through the same process.

Imagine what this shock must do to the brain.

The only mercy for the baby (and the brain) is amnesia—shock-based unconsciousness.

IN 1997, I was jarred by my own amnesia. This didn't happen gently, like the soft kiss of a prince but came on violently—in an explosive rush of life.

"PUSH. PUSH! PUSH!" came the collective scream of one doctor, three nurses, and my husband, his booming baritone firing into my left ear.

My knees were forced up to my underarms and contractions rolled thunder from my belly. The doctor pushed at my most tender place with such force her nails cut through latex and left half-moon incisions.

The whole scene was pandemonium with focus. My son wasn't born as much as he was commanded into our midst.

Me? After four days of labor with no sleep and no food, I was eager to get him out too. I pushed!

When my son finally emerged, all became quiet—as if a pause button had been pressed. Look at him waving his arms and kicking his feet, his face scrunched in a grimace of glorious outrage.

I cradled him close to my chest and entered into that universe of mother and child.

He warbled his first sounds that were cries of indignation and I whispered how everything was going to be okay. I made note of how perfect he was, how powerful and wise for one so small. I was like every other mother throughout time, touching fingers and toes, but before I could finish my count, a nurse popped our bubble by explaining the baby needed to be assessed—standard procedure for a baby born six weeks early.

I was hesitant to give him up but I was also in a pretty compromising position. See me on the delivery table, legs spread far too wide to be considered appropriate, blood everywhere, and those overhead floodlights that left no room for imagination.

At that same moment, the doctor, eager to deliver the placenta, pressed on my belly. There was a splash and out came a rush of water that made the doctor jump back. "What in the world?" she asked.

In a flash, the nurse lifted the baby off my chest like a seasoned waitress taking away an empty plate and was gone before I could protest, "Hey, bring that back, I'm not done!" Worse, the doctor pushed up her sleeve and reached inside my body without even asking. As she screwed up her face and considered the ceiling in concentration, she also patted around inside like she had lost a ring in my uterus.

Did I mention the pain?

Yes, all this hurt like hell, most of my body—especially down there—was on fire. I wanted to beat this woman in retribution and scream at her to get her goddamned arm out of me. I was also steamed that my kid was gone.

The doctor pulled out and made an educated guess. "Looks like you were pregnant with twins," she said. "There's no fetus now but obviously the bag has been there all this time. No wonder your baby came early."

There was laughter among the hospital staff.

Another baby? Did he or she die? I blinked on a moment of sadness—a lump formed in my throat. Poor baby.

The nurses called out their reports: "Good color. Strong lungs. Nice reflexes. A first-rate heartbeat."

My son was given a score—eight and nine on a scale used to determine good health. Ten was the best.

The baby cried and I felt the surprising tug of his need in my heart. "Give him back to me," I said.

The edge in my voice had my husband give me a look that said, "That wasn't very polite." The doctor even raised her eyebrows.

Was there such a thing as delivery room etiquette? Had I missed the memo?

I slapped at my husband to get off his chair and get the baby, since obviously I could not. He jumped into action and headed over to the corner, but before he could take over, one of the nurses had our child bundled like a to-go order of ribs. "We're going to need to do more tests," she stated. "We'll bring him back soon."

It was work but I shimmied myself up to my elbows, winching at the mind-bending pain. "More tests?" I asked. "Why? You just said he was great."

The doctor pressed a firm hand at my pelvis as if to remind me to stay put. "It's procedure," the doctor said. "Don't worry, you'll get him back."

Another round of laughter passed through the staff as if she had made the best joke, but my sense of humor was not tuned to the medical establishment and these incomprehensible rules. I was a mother now. I wanted my child.

The baby fussed and the nurse patted at his back as if he was hers.

I sent my husband my best "If you don't get that baby, I'll kill you" look. My eyebrows pulled together, my jaw was tight, and my eyes went narrow.

As he reached out, yet again attempting to fulfill my primal wishes, the nurse shooed him away. She said something about hospital rules and my being overly emotional.

Poor man, he lifted his empty hands and shrugged his shoulders.

On his face was an expression of utter bafflement. Among all these women, the man was out of his element.

Between us, we had already talked about the possibility of the baby being separated from me. If something was wrong once the baby was born, our back-up plan was to make sure he stayed with the baby—no matter what.

My husband bit his lip, unsure if our back-up plan was still in place, so I was the one who said it out loud:

"I want my husband to carry him."

A feeling of hesitation filled the room, confusion too. These people weren't used to a mother calling the shots. The doctor did her own little nod of ascent and the nurse finally handed over the baby.

My husband, a little awkward, took our son into his arms.

"Watch his neck. Support his head," I commanded, as if I was an expert on babies.

My husband adjusted his hands and three nurses swarmed.

What if something happened? What if these doctors made a mistake?

"Stay with him!" I called out.

"I will," my husband said.

"Don't leave his side."

"I won't."

As the door closed, I eased back into the pillows again and looked between my legs. The doctor was a woman but she behaved like a man—professional and detached.

"Do you have children?" I asked.

She laughed like having a child would be the last thing she would ever do and shook her head.

I directed my attention to the ceiling and chastised myself for being difficult and defensive and making all this worse than it was but I couldn't help myself. I was so scared. What was happening to my son?

And that is when it happened. I began to awaken from a life-long slumber.

As if time had split in half, I was back in 1963. I saw my own mother—helpless on a table. I saw myself being brutally separated from her. I felt a rush of intense emotion—shame mixed with fury.

And then I felt myself being dragged from her by unforgiving strangers. I felt sensations of movement that were swift and certain.

A series of jagged flashbacks took over then and flooded my senses: white light in my field of vision, laughing murmuring voices in my ears, and in my stomach there was a turn of nausea.

While being stitched up, I began to shake. My arms and legs were out of my control.

The doctor called out for the nurse and soon I was covered with warm blankets. I heard someone say I was in shock from giving birth and then I lost consciousness.

THREE

THE GIFT FROM GOD

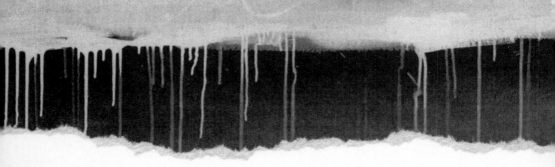

AFTER BEING TAKEN FROM CATHERINE, I was deposited in the nursery at St. Mary's Hospital.

Bud and Janet got a call from their doctor, a man named Smernoff, not long after he had washed his hands of my mother.

Although Dr. Smernoff is dead now, he is on record as saying he delivered 6,200 babies between 1929 and 1974. How many infants were taken in the way I was taken from my own mother? How many of us were given away on his advice?

"SHE'S WAITING," SMERNOFF told Bud on the phone, as if I was at the hospital and tapping my foot.

According to family lore, Bud was Smernoff's accountant. Smernoff's daughter went to school with Bud's younger sister and the two families were longtime friends. They went to the same cocktail parties, danced with each other's wives, and shared stories over plates of barbeque.

Dr. Smernoff pulled strings to get Bud and Janet off a three-year adoption waiting list. He told the Catholic agency that in his opinion, the Laucks were special people and he recommended them with no hesitation. He didn't mention Janet's medical problems, which included a recent surgery to remove an eleven-inch tumor from her spine, a history of hallucinations, lacerated ulcers in her stomach, and kidney failure. He didn't talk about Bud's financial ruin, due to Janet's medical bills.

The adoption was approved.

BUD AND JANET couldn't get to me right away. I'm not sure why the time lapsed but there is a story of how they had a bowling match to attend that had been scheduled months in advance (Bud was an accomplished bowler with trophies on the mantel of their home). I also remember hearing there was childcare to arrange for their older child—a boy named Bryan—and that there was shopping to do in order to pick up diapers, a crib, and bottles.

Two days after I was born, they arrived at St. Mary's and I was passed into Janet's arms. "This one is a real handful," the nurse warned, as if my incessant crying had gotten on her nerves.

Janet asked after the purple welts that were spread over the top of my head. "Forceps delivery," the nurse said. "Very stubborn baby."

This brief conversation became Lauck legend. I was defined as a "handful" and "stubborn" throughout childhood. My Auntie Carol used to say, "You are the most willful child I have ever met." When I was small, I'd stay at Auntie Carol's house and in no time, she'd position me in a corner between the living room and the front room. I'd spend hours with my nose against plaster studying the intersection of two right angles. Auntie Carol told me to think hard about my stubborn nature. She suggested I change my ways.

BUD'S FULL NAME was Joseph Everett Lauck. He was a tall, clean-cut man with brown eyes and hair. His shoulders were sloped and he stooped from the waist, as if to apologize for his height.

Janet was Janet Lee Ferrel and stood about five foot three. Her hair and eyes were almost black. Her complexion was quite fair.

Bud was an accountant who started his own firm in Carson City. As a young man in university, he did not attend lectures and still aced his exams. He was called a genius.

Janet was a homemaker whose ambition centered on family. She went to college, majored in art and modeled clothing for department stores. She was called elegant and glamorous.

Bud was the eldest son in a family of five children. He was raised Catholic. He had a reckless side—he drove too fast and liked to gamble. He also dreamed of being a millionaire by the time he was forty years old. His hero was Playboy magnate Hugh Hefner.

Janet was the oldest in her family of three kids. Her people were Methodists. Since childhood, Janet had been frail and sickly but she didn't admit her condition to anyone. When she was "out of sorts," as she called it, she kept any residual discomfort to herself and took handfuls of aspirin to manage her pain. "A lady doesn't complain," she used to say.

To JANET, I was considered a gift from God and the answer to her prayers for good health. She was sure she wouldn't be given a baby if she were going to die. My arrival felt mystic and important—my place in their world, as daughter, was called destiny.

I wanted to believe I could be someone's destiny. I liked to imagine I was of the divine. I went so far as to build rough scaffolding that propped me up on the set of their lives where I tottered around as if I belonged, but if pressed I would admit I felt itchy and wrong, as if I wore a pair of tights that were too small and hung below my crotch. My life was like a series of tugs and pulls where I had to take huge, wide steps across my interior rooms in order to fit, and still I did not find myself at home in their world. Perhaps the reason for this has to do with time. In the end, I had so little of it with Janet, Bud, and Bryan.

FOUR

THREE DEATHS

JANET DIED WHEN I WAS seven years old. Bud died eighteen months later, when I was nine. Bryan ended his life when I was twenty. He was twenty-three.

For many years of my adult life, I snapped off this news in precise sentences whittled to the most basic facts. Having grown up to become an investigative television reporter and trained in the art of story telling, presentation, and delivery, I'd developed the belief that to tell it straight was the best approach. Why be elusive or even coy?

Life had been brutal to me and I'd go ahead and be brutal in return.

Dead, buried, gone.

That's how I coped with all that loss and if you asked I'd tell you that I didn't look back. I'd say, "It happened, it's over, I'm past all that."

For the most part, people believed me and didn't ask me to elaborate on the gruesome details.

If they had, I would have been just as succinct: Janet died from complications associated with a tumor in her spine, Bud had an unexpected heart attack, and Bryan shot himself in the head.

This usually had folks take a step or two back, giving me room, as if my situation had some form of residual effect. Was tragedy contagious?

Before people went too far away, I was quick to reassure that I was doing just great. *Look at me,* I practically said. *Look at what I have become!*

I was the one who offered to shake hands first when introductions took place. I was the one who asked a man out—not the other way around.

I was the one who didn't need anyone, who left the party first, and who was alone even when in a crowd of people.

I was a survivor, yes, but I didn't want to be known as a survivor. I wanted to be known as the one with ambition to spare. I wanted you to see me as a busy person with important matters to think about.

Feelings?

What were feelings?

Who needed them?

As soon as my son, Spencer, was given a clean bill of health and we were released from the hospital, we went home and every known emotion welled to the surface.

Before the baby, I had been tough, focused, sharp, and defined by my ambitions. After the baby, as I lay in the quiet of those lush days of sleep, breastfeeding, and skin-to-skin contact, I became primal mother—overflowing with a new desire to nurture and protect. I was also molten, raw, Technicolor love—this kaleidoscope of infatuation and devotion. And I was scared, paranoid, bitchy, unreasonable, and argumentative.

Here was my son, his warm body draped heavily on my chest after a drunken feast on my ample milk supply, and I found myself looking at him but also looking beyond him into the abyss of my own childhood and infancy. At times there would be great swells of sadness, loneliness, fear, and confusion. Other times, I would hear fragments of sound, experience splinters of recollection, and feel shards of sensation. Sometimes it felt as if madness circled overhead, not unlike the teddy bear mobile that spun above Spencer's crib.

EXPERTS DIAGNOSED ME with postpartum depression and in part, that may have been correct, but it felt bigger than depression.

I was now feeling everything, and therefore, it became important to sort my feelings out.

This is when I began to write the book that would become my first, *Blackbird*. Just prior, there had been a spate of therapy but talking all this insanity out with someone who charged by the hour seemed ludicrous—and time consuming. I'd be in therapy until I was eighty. I didn't have that kind of time! Spencer didn't have that kind of time.

Instead I used my reporting skills to investigate Janet's death,

Bud's death, and then Bryan's death. I wrote everything I could remember and told myself that I did this writing, not for my sake, but for Spencer's. He deserved a mother who was fully awakened and not a hostage to her past. He also deserved a historical account that hadn't been reduced to a series of sound bites. Spencer, I told myself, deserved the full truth.

FIVE

GYPSY TRASH

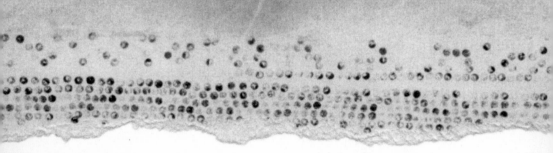

"HERE'S THE TRUTH," Bryan said. "Your real parents threw you in the trash."

It was a sunny day in Hermosa Beach, California, in 1970. Our family, still intact at this time, had moved from Nevada a year earlier so Janet could get the best health care at UCLA Medical Center.

I was seven years old. Bryan was nearly ten.

It had been an ordinary day, like any other—school, peanut butter sandwiches, milk to wash it down, skinned knees, Barbie dolls, and episodes of *The Brady Bunch*. And then Bryan said, "You're adopted. Your parents were gypsies. They tossed you in the trash."

I remember standing on the sidewalk in front of our apartment that had a view of the sea. Gulls hung in the sky like ornaments with no wires. Salted wind blew off the Pacific Ocean.

BY SEVEN, I had adapted quite nicely, thank you very much. As the designated special gift from God, I took up my role as divine caregiver with an earnestness that might be called either saintly or irritat- ing. I didn't really care what others thought of me though, I was my mother's savior and Lord did I have a lot of work to do.

Janet was such a sick woman, most of her time was spent in bed where she withered away. Kidneys, bladder, bowel, liver, and stom- ach—all were put under strain by the persistent growth that lived in her spine. Although it wasn't cancer in the way one thinks of cancer, it was a tumor and when it grew, it pressed on nerves and brought dreadful pain.

Many medications were prescribed and in the same way that some software programs will not interact well inside your computer, her medications did not interact well within her body. Pain meds brought on hallucination. Antihallucinogens brought emotional pitches. Other drugs had her sleep and sleep and sleep. Add in a few surgeries to remove a kidney and to scrape out bits of the reoccurring tumor and you get the picture. Janet was dying.

BRYAN MAY HAVE been so cruel in handling this news of my adoption based on a need to put me in my place. Perhaps he was jealous of my position of importance as divine interloper. How I wish I could have told him he need not feel such pettiness. Obviously, I was failing in my celestial work, and besides, it was no good night of sleep being me—the twenty-four-hour worry, the changing of the urine bag that connected to her catheter, the endless filling and refilling of her water glass, in hopes that each sip she took would turn her health around. The guilt. The gut-wrenching realization that I was not saving this woman but might actually be causing harm due to incompetence. Janet needed hospitalization—not the care of a child—and yet I tried so hard. I believed I had some otherworldly power to heal.

But Bryan, by nature, was a pissed-off kid. Anger was one of his defining qualities. There was good in there too but his light was hard to see through the darkness of his rage.

When he told me I was adopted, I felt dirty and bad—the opposite of God's gift. In his declaration, "You're adopted and gypsy trash," I became a fallen angel.

In an act of recklessness, I raced into our apartment, slammed the front door and locked him out as if this might make what he said untrue.

Bryan banged his fists on the door and bellowed, "Let me in! Let me in!"

Despite a feeling of pure terror, I dragged a stool across the kitchen and under the phone that was screwed into the wall. Climbing up and getting myself steady, I tugged the handset from the cradle and dialed my father at work.

There were no push buttons in this day. Each number required a spin of a rotary dial, which took a month of Sundays to my own hard beating heart. Bryan's banging became louder still. The door rattled under the power of his fists.

Finally, my father picked up on the other line and when he did, I began to cry and talk at the same time. "Bryan says I'm adopted," I said in a rush. "He says my parents are gypsies and they put me in the trash."

A long moment of stony silence passed and then my father said he was coming home from work early. Something he never did.

IN THE HALL of our apartment, there was an unused place to toss extra shoes and hang winter coats. I wedged into the corner of that hall closet with my Barbie suitcase against my chest. I pushed my feet against the door, to keep it shut and sat very still.

My father and Bryan watched TV.

My mother slept, as she always did, in her room.

And I there I sat, undone.

My father had come home right away from work to give over the details. He said they had wanted a daughter; actually Janet had wanted a daughter most of all. When she couldn't have more children—being so sick and all—well, they adopted me. He told me that my first mother was a young girl in trouble. It was a long time ago, in Reno, and that was all he knew.

In part, I felt such relief. It was as if I had been freed from the lie we were all living and taken off the stage. It was okay not to be God's gift in the light of this news and my days of adapting felt as if they might be nearing an end. Another Jennifer was out there, another life to be lived.

I wanted to ask if he knew my mother's name.

I wanted to know where she lived.

I even felt like saying, "No hard feelings but this whole adoption thing isn't working out so great for me. I want to go home now."

But my father didn't entertain conversation. These were the

days of children being seen and not heard. Speaking up was called back talk.

Once the news was out there, my father looked tired and old. He said it was time to have dinner and thus ended our "adoption talk."

I felt that he wanted everything to be as it was before—as if the adoption didn't matter—but such a scenario wasn't possible.

I was like one of those fake snakes that had exploded from a faux can of nuts, the gag gift any child can purchase in a prank joke store. In Bryan's declaration and my father's confirmation, I had been freed from my own confining space and learned how I was someone else's child with a story beyond Janet's rotting sickness, Bryan's seething anger, and Bud's long days of work. These people were living *their* lives, not mine. My life was out there, somewhere.

But since my father wasn't going to talk this out and help me sort the story, I had to figure it out myself. That's when I slipped into the closet, covert and quiet. I plotted my escape.

As THE LIGHT of the setting sun fell through the slats of the closet door, I opened the lid of the Barbie suitcase and dumped out doll clothes, Malibu Suntan Barbie, and a few pairs of plastic shoes. The junk tumbled over suede loafers and patent leather pumps.

By my estimation, the little case could hold a couple pair of underwear, an extra pair of pants, and a sweater. I'd put the rest of my clothes on and head out the door.

I told myself that maybe the trouble had passed for my first mother and first father. Maybe they wanted me back. I could see myself in Reno, standing in front of Harrah's casino and surveying the main drag. But then my vision faded and it was just me in the closet again.

I asked myself some very adult questions next: *How in the world are you going to make your way to Reno? What if your real parents aren't there anymore? And—think about this—what if they don't want you back?*

It is said that an adopted child has two identities—that of being the child who has adapted to the family where she has been placed, and that of being a shadow baby of the mother who gave her life. The baby part is waiting to be fully born. The growing child is conforming and shaping and bending to fit the adoptive family in order to ensure a secure place.

I distinctly felt these two worlds at play within my small body on that day in the closet. I had been awakened to the reality of another life—yet to be lived—and I was also forced to accept, for my very survival, that I could not yet access that original life.

A FEW MONTHS later, Janet died. The date was September 19, 1971. This was Bryan's birthday. Like me, my brother lost his mother on the day he was born—only ten years later.

I hurt for him in a way that couldn't be spoken. It was empathy. I knew something about how Bryan felt on that hard day.

JANET AND I never spoke about the adoption or that I had been told the truth.

When she died, I felt great empathy for Bryan but I did not feel sad the way many children do when they lose their mothers. Grief came inevitably; it was actually expected. But for me sadness was not the first emotion. At the age of seven, I felt defeat. Janet's death became my first failure. I had been God's gift and had let her down.

SIX

COME LOOK

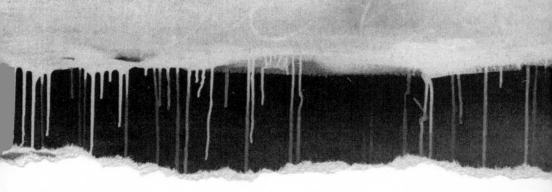

IT'S FUNNY THE way we lock our stories down in the past and walk away, as if memory will be obedient and stay put. I've learned, the hard way, that it doesn't work like that. Unless you are Peter Pan, the shadow you cast stays pretty close to your heels.

As my son Spencer grew into a fine little boy—fast smile, curious mind, and an eagerness to take things apart and reassemble them again—I tripped in and out of the canyons of memory and excavated quite a bit of my story. I typed everything on the page. Mornings were walks to the bagel store at the top of the hill, afternoons found us on park swings, and evenings were for splashing together in the hot tub, eating dinner, building LEGOs, and reading books. During naps and early in the morning, I wrote my life. Next to being a mother to Spencer, writing into the past was my job.

As my husband traveled a lot, in fact most of those first three years, it was just Spence and I.

It seems a little odd to say it this way but Spencer and I were like best friends—or maybe twins. He was the baby I delivered and I had become the phantom baby I had carried in my own mystery bag of water. I had given birth to myself in the form of a shadow—a ghost—and now, Spencer and I were growing together.

WHEN SPENCER WAS four years old, I had my daughter—wispy blond hair, heart-shaped face, and eyes that were a dove-soft shade of medium blue that might be called gray. I named her Josephine Catherine.

Where Spencer's birth had been urgent and scary, Jo arrived in a state of relative calm. She was two weeks late. I hired an unruffled doctor who told me to take my time pushing and I watched Jo enter the world thanks to a mirror positioned near the end of the bed.

Once my daughter was born, we were apart for just seconds and then she remained in my arms for most of the next several years. On our first night together, she stayed in my room, ten pounds of sleeping baby snuggled close to my side, and I found myself studying the shadows of our hospital room.

I was taken back to that day Bryan told me I had been adopted. I thought of that young girl my father had told me about, the one he said had "gotten in trouble" by being pregnant with me.

Before having my own daughter, I hadn't allowed myself to give much thought to that person—that birth mother. I had told myself that she really didn't matter much to my story. After all, the biggest part of the past was what I could remember, right? I told myself that what mattered most had been the deaths of my family and the years of striving to survive.

In the way that Spencer's birth began my awakening process, Jo's birth continued to unfold my psyche and reveal the many dimensions of truth. My thoughts now jumped from their rigid linear tracks and swirled like currents of air to become like a dance, or a prayer, or maybe even a song.

My first mother felt very important to me in light of Josephine Catherine. Jo was a link in the lineage of women that connected me to my mother and my mother to her mother and on back through the generations. I wanted to tell my mystery mother, that troubled young girl from so long ago, that Josephine was here—a granddaughter. I wanted to say, "Come look!"

SEVEN

KARMA

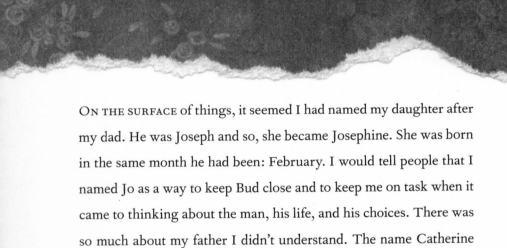

ON THE SURFACE of things, it seemed I had named my daughter after my dad. He was Joseph and so, she became Josephine. She was born in the same month he had been: February. I would tell people that I named Jo as a way to keep Bud close and to keep me on task when it came to thinking about the man, his life, and his choices. There was so much about my father I didn't understand. The name Catherine was just a favorite I carried around through childhood, a fancy and a secret.

AFTER JANET'S FUNERAL in 1971, my father moved us to L.A., and we lived in a sprawling bungalow with a wide porch, hardwood floors, built-in cabinets, and an impossible number of rooms and floors.

The owner of the house was a woman who had three children. She was known as a divorcée.

At first, the divorcée was just a friend. Soon she was upgraded to my father's fiancée. Then she became his wife.

This transition took place within six months of Janet's death.

What of loyalty?

What of grief?

What of the mourning period?

AUNTIE CAROL CAME to visit us in L.A., just before hasty nuptials were exchanged. She wanted to meet this new woman and had a plan to clean out the old apartment in Hermosa Beach.

Auntie Carol dragged me along as assistant—she said the work would do me good.

AUNTIE CAROL WAS my father's older sister and was an awesome no-nonsense presence—a powerhouse of full-bodied womanhood with thick thighs and a wide behind. Her breasts were so huge, they were like lampshades under her sweater. When she walked, her steps made the earth move and her voice was a booming drum that rattled the bones.

Auntie Carol was also considered a bit of a mystic. She read Tarot cards and palms. My cousins said she could see the future.

The woman scared me to death.

DURING OUR DAY of scrubbing and sorting, the apartment was bleached free of our smells, and our clothes, toys, and household goods were sorted into storage boxes. While we worked, Auntie Carol talked. She said my father wanted to put the past in the past and move on with his life. She said it was good he had a healthy woman to love. And she said that Janet had been sick for all of their marriage—which had taken a toll on him.

"He deserves a little happiness," I remember her saying, as if my father had been very unhappy before.

WHEN THE JOB was done and it was time to go back to the divorcée-landlord-fiancée's house, Auntie Carol gave me a few treasures: Bud and Janet's wedding album, Janet's wedding ring, and a necklace of perfectly matched freshwater pearls.

I did not want these things. I told Auntie Carol to give the stuff to Bryan. "He's her son," I added.

In the old days, Auntie Carol would have swatted my butt and pressed my willful face into a corner but on that day, she seemed almost impressed.

"Look," she said, "if I wanted to give these things to Bryan, I would have. I am giving them to you because you are the daughter."

I eyed her with a look that said I wasn't the daughter and she knew it. Again, Auntie Carol paused. She must have realized that I knew I was adopted.

She cleared her throat and pulled herself up.

"You listen to me little girl. You *are* the daughter," she said, "and it's your job to remember your mother."

To remember was an intriguing and even tantalizing assignment. I thought, *I can do that! I can remember.*

Auntie Carol, without the benefit of Tarot or palm, had predicted my future.

My father's new wife had a name. I won't write it here. Nor will I write the names of her children.

The stepmother I will call Deb, and her kids I will call Christopher, Veronica, and Kendall. I'll say Veronica and Kendall were twins, just a few days older than me and were like wild alley cats— red hair and freckles everywhere.

I'll say Christopher was fourteen years old with curly blond hair and was skinny and pale, as if he had been sick.

Deb was like every evil stepmother in every fairytale I have ever read. She was skinny with wide bony hips and a flat, unimpressive chest. Her face was long and narrow too. She was downright unattractive but that's not how other people remembered her.

I have been told she was pretty and quite smart.

At eight, I didn't see it. I considered Deb to be a major step down.

My mother had been Jackie Kennedy.

Deb was a cross between a haggard Jane Fonda and perhaps an older version of Jennifer Beals in *Flashdance*—headbands, leg warmers, and big sweatshirts that hung below her hips.

My mother had been patient, gentle, and kind. I don't remember her ever being angry or cruel—especially to a child.

Deb seemed to go out of her way to be cruel, which was likely the result of a distressing childhood of her own, but when I was eight years old I wasn't considering the woman's psychological profile. That wasn't my job.

My father's state of mind was my primary concern and the only explanation I could find was one I had borrowed from the fairytale

Snow White. That father, the king, had lost his beloved queen and in a mind-bending state of ruinous grief, he married the evil step-mother. I concluded that my own father, in the same predicament as the king, had temporarily lost his mind.

BRYAN DID NOT fit into the new family. Now and then, Christopher, Kendall, and Veronica included him in their trio but then they'd turn against him with a snide comment or a collective snub. No matter what approach Bryan tried—as bully, as charmer, as cooperative player—he was never accepted.

Deb called him fat and inferior and fed her contempt to her children. They gobbled it up and called him fat too.

In order to cope, Bryan took refuge in music. Led Zeppelin became a favorite band. He wore bubble headphones that made him look like a bug and disappeared into lyric and sound.

BY 1973, WE had moved from the big house in L.A. to a house in Fountain Valley and then to a house in Huntington Beach. By the time I was nine years old, I was given a bedroom set from the catalogue pages of Sears. My room became a fairytale of white furniture with gold trim, a canopy bed, and every shade of pink for the curtains and bedspread.

In this sacred place, I discovered sanctuary and the power of solitude. I listened to soundtracks from *West Side Story* and *Fiddler on the Roof*—two of my favorite movies. I also listened to my father's old Cat Stevens's tapes and learned all the words to "Morning Has

Broken," "Peace Train," and "Wild World." I was crazy for The Beatles and The Jackson 5. Soon I discovered books that had been recorded on albums. *The Lorax, The Sneetches, Yertle the Turtle, Horton Hears a Who,* and *Green Eggs and Ham.* Holding a book, I'd follow along with the narrator's voice and like magic, random letters became words and words shaped sentences. Paragraphs emerged and knitted themselves into chapters. Finally, whole stories revealed themselves and I gained entry into a world that would serve me for the rest of my life. Reading.

ON DECEMBER 4, 1973, my father had a heart attack.

No one saw it coming.

He was just gone.

Deb said it was my father's own fault. She said the word "karma" at a time when very few people were using that term. "He had wished such a death on his business partner," she said. "It was karma."

KARMA IS DEFINED as a noun and is often interpreted as "fate." In the eastern sensibility, the word *karma* is Sanskrit for action as well as for cause and effect. Karma—when you really look at it—is a verb. Cause and effect are active principles—changing constantly and largely impacted by the focal point of "intent."

Philosophers, scholars, and great masters will debate, for hours, the issue of karma. Understanding karma is a jumping off point for some of the greatest mystic teachings. I know, I've been there listening to these teachings and have taken copious notes. I likely became a student of the word "karma" in order to scour all evidence of Deb's perspective from my own thinking like one scrapes the remains of a splattered bug from a windshield.

And yet Deb remains one of my most vivid teachers. When a lesson really sinks in, it is usually the result of a hard moment in life that has been fully brought to light. Deb blaming my father's death on karma was one of these moments.

Let me imagine my father did wish a heart-attack death on his business partner. Let me invent a scene between my father and Deb, in their marital bedroom with rumpled sheets and whispered pillow talk after the five kids were asleep, and he says, "I hate my business partner, I wish he'd just die."

If he did say such a thing, did he truly intend for his business partner to die? Did he go on, after he was out of their bed and dressed for his day, to strategize a way to induce a heart attack in his partner?

I certainly didn't know my father well, but he was no killer. The man loved the ocean and longed for his own sailboat. He was searching for meaning and security. He listened to the songs of Cat Stevens.

My father was flawed—all human beings are. But I'm pretty sure his death wasn't the result of a bad feeling, or even a dark statement made about a business partner.

I'm quite sure my father did not intend for his words to be used as a sword against his own children either.

It is likely that my father died from years of bad thoughts, heavy thoughts, worried thoughts, and more, the mounting debt that took him further away from his dream of being a millionaire by the time he was forty.

My father died when he was thirty-nine years old.

EIGHT

THE LESSON

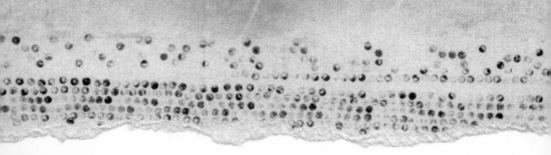

"HOW MUCH DO YOU love me?" Spencer asks.

"I love you over the moon, around each and every star, and back to planet earth where I turn over every rock until I find you," I say.

"How much do you love me?" Josephine asks.

"Well, I love you up to the sun, down a rainbow, all the way to the bottom of the ocean, through a meadow of wildflowers, and into the center of your heart," I say.

By the time Spencer is ten and Jo is five—this is how it goes—the two of them want to know how much I love them again and again and then one more time. I have crafted little tales of my love to fit their unique personalities. Spencer has a penchant for playing hide and seek and he loves space travel. Jo has become an artist who draws and paints landscapes that include sunshine, oceans, rainbows, and flowers.

When we all lay together at night, reading our books and drinking pots of mint tea that Jo makes from the garden out front, they ask me these questions about love as if my answer will change.

"Do you love Spencer more?" Jo asks.

"No."

"I know you love Jo more than you love me," Spencer tries.

"Not true," I say.

They look at each other across my body. Jo is under my left arm, Spencer is under my right, and they are just sure, this time, I'm going to slip.

"Come on," Spencer says, "Jo was the easier baby."

"That's true," Jo nods.

"Nope, not easier, different."

"But Spencer didn't sleep like I did," Jo counters.

"He slept enough," I say. "And sleep doesn't equal love."

"I know you love her more because she does better art," Spencer says.

"Not true," I say.

"You love him more because he was first," Jo points out.

Finally, I laugh out loud because they are so funny and silly and deluded!

"To say I love one of you more than the other is like saying my left arm is better than my right, or that I like one leg better than the other. I love you both. Both of you are essential."

Finally, they are satisfied (or they just give up) and we move on with the routine of reading and drawing and drinking more tea. It's another night of my family being my family.

I LOVED MY father but not as a child loves a parent. I loved him in a protective, *I'll-take-care-of-you* kind of way. I loved him like a mother. I loved him like a hopeful lover. (In fact, I wanted my father to wait for me to grow up so I could marry him. I wanted to prove to him that I would be a good wife. Was this the guilt that came from believing I had failed in my task of being a gift from God?)

I was obsessed with molding myself to be my father's ideal. I set aside my fear of the ocean to go sailing with him, I tried to learn how to swim (despite my fear of water) to please him, and I ran on a competitive track team, winning trophies and medals because this is what he wanted. I detested running and could never get enough breath.

My relationship with my father was defined by adaptations designed to impress him and still he remained a detached ideal.

Looking back at Jennifer, that little girl with such adult burdens, I finally understand how my father and I were simply two souls thrown together by circumstance. His wife wanted another child (specifically a daughter) and he pulled some strings to fulfill her desire. I was like a handbag or a scarf. Any baby would have done. It wasn't personal.

In the end, we were strangers to each other. There were no markers of genetics or lineage between us. Our primary bond was shared time and shared tragedy.

ON THE NIGHT my father died, I dreamt he was in my room, going through my dresser drawers, as if in search of something left behind. The next morning, I thought about the dream for a long time and in light of the news that he was gone—at least in body—I knew it wasn't a dream at all. My father had been in my room, searching.

What had he been looking for? What did he want? Was he attempting to pack me up and set me on a path that would take me far away from Deb? Had love, pure love, finally entered into our story? Was he trying, too late, to set things right?

ABOUT A YEAR after my father died, Deb got it into her head that she was going to be a healer for her church. She secured an apartment for herself and her own children, sent Bryan off somewhere (I have no idea where), and I was farmed out to a communal house in central L.A.

As she dumped me with my princess bedroom set and a few bucks, Deb said it was time I learned to be on my own. "You are a challenge to the family dynamic," she explained. "This arrangement will teach you the obligatory skills of autonomy."

Each morning, I was expected to work in the kitchen and help make breakfast. Then I was to go to school at Hoover Street Elementary. After school, I had another job at her church, cleaning offices, and then I was to get back to the commune and help with dinner.

The woman kept me busy and apparently collected and retained my wages from behind the scenes.

I was eleven years old.

FOUR MONTHS PASSED while I learned the obligatory skills of autonomy. I was alive and I was surviving but I was also terrified and began to hear voices in my head—a chorus of mocking insanity, a murmuring sound with laughter in the background. I could make the voices stop, but only by singing out loud. Snappy, energetic tunes worked best, such as "If I Were a Rich Man" or "When You're a Jet."

I was a walking minstrel. Lunatic child.

When I wasn't singing at the top of my lungs, I was talking to myself. I'd say, "It's going to be okay, you're going to be fine."

IN THE LOW valley of what I considered my darkest time, nearly homeless, crazy, and parentless, I witnessed a miracle.

One of the women, who also lived in the house, was having a baby in her room.

I had been invited.

I remember standing near the end of table, one of several witnesses. The woman, perhaps in her twenties, was moaning and rolling her head from side to side. She had a honey complexion and light reddish hair. Spiral curls of her hair stuck in the sweat that covered her forehead and neck.

Her husband was at her side, holding her hand.

There was great anticipation in the room. Sunlight fell through the tall windows and sent rectangles over the table, the floor, and the walls.

When it was time for her to push, a midwife spoke in hushed tones—encouraging and reassuring.

The Beatles' *White Album* was on the table and "Blackbird" played on the turntable.

Amidst the birdcalls at the end of the song, not one baby was born, but rather, two. Twins!

As the small ones were lifted out—bare naked and squirming with life—something in me shifted.

The voices in my head were gone. All fear had dissolved.

I could hear my own breath moving in and out of my body and I remember looking down at my own hands, touching my fingers together as if seeing myself for the first time.

I was in that room, vivid and alert, but I was also beyond that room.

It wasn't like I didn't feel all the feelings I used to feel—anger at Deb, confusion about my situation, sadness for the death of my parents, longing, loneliness, and fear. Those feelings were with me but had been diluted to become small and unimportant when placed in the sea of this larger feeling.

It was awakening.

NINE

RETIREMENT

BY THE SUMMER of 1975, Deb was finally busted for the way she was (or wasn't) taking care of Bryan and me. An intervention of sorts took place—orchestrated by an aunt and uncle from Janet's side of the family. Accusations of neglect and abuse were leveled at Deb and pretty soon the Lauck side of the family mobilized as well.

Bryan was sent to live in Carson City with Janet's people— Aunt Georgia and Uncle Charles—and I came to live with Bud's parents—Grandma Maggie and Grandpa Ed.

GRANDMA AND GRANDPA had a double-wide at the Sunset Mobile Home Park—one of hundreds that were lined up like building blocks on the side of a dusty Reno hill.

Each day I lived with my grandparents, I'd amble down to the swimming pool that overlooked the city. I'd sit at the edge, kick my feet in the clear water, and study the long snake of the Reno freeway. Cars and trucks raced back and forth. I could see the Reno skyline too—casinos, office buildings, and neighborhoods with houses and schools and parks.

Hot wind would sweep over me and I'd lean forward from my chest as if I meant to fly off the edge of that pool and swoop down to the city. The tug was magnetic but I didn't know what to do with the sensation. I just felt this need to go down into Reno. I could almost imagine walking—like someone asleep and stumbling wherever I was supposed to go.

It was Catherine of course. She lived down there. She was now twenty-eight years old. She had two children of her own.

In my file, at Catholic Charities, it was noted that Janet and Bud had died and that I was living with my grandparents. I'm not sure how that information got into my file or who reported it.

While I idled my day away at the pool, Grandpa would play golf and Grandma would stay at the trailer, reading a paperback romance.

Just before four, I'd wander back up to the trailer again, Grandpa would come home, and Grandma would put her book away.

Cocktail hour went from four to five-thirty—they'd have vodka on the rocks and I'd get ginger ale—and we all watched *Merv Griffin* and *The CBS News with Walter Cronkite*.

By six, we'd have dinner, watch the evening movie, and eat a bowl of ice cream—vanilla with chocolate sauce on top. Grandpa read *Golf Magazine*. Grandma finished her book. At ten, we all went to bed.

They called this life being retired.

AT NIGHT, AS I lay on the fold-out bed in the guest room, I created a dream where I finished childhood at the Sunset Mobile Home Park. I saw myself go to high school and then college. Details about what I might want to study or even become later in life were beyond my reach. I was too tired to imagine a future. I felt as old as Grandma and Grandpa. I felt older in fact. The way I saw things, I was retired too.

NEAR THE END of that summer, we all sat down for dinner in the dining room and the view was of the Sierra Mountains and the sunset. The sky was on fire.

Grandma announced that Bryan was going to move to Oklahoma and that I was moving to a military complex nearby called Stead. We were being parceled out to Bud's younger siblings.

"It's all set," Grandma said.

Grandma was a tiny woman who wore tropical print dresses she called muumuus. She had a million wrinkles that webbed over her face and down her neck. Even her lips were creased.

I hadn't even tasted my chicken noodle soup. My spoon was mid-lift. I set the spoon down on my napkin and put my shaking hands in my lap. "I thought I could just stay here with you," I said.

Grandma rested her elbows on the table and wrung her hands together. She looked from me to Grandpa and back to me.

"We'd love to have you stay, Jenny," Grandpa piped in, rescuing Grandma. "But you need young people. You need a family."

Grandpa was just like my father. His nose was bigger but they shared the same wide grin and fast laugh.

"Did I do something wrong?" I asked. "Is that why I have to go?"

"No, no," Grandma said. She reached across the dining table to console me. She had skin like tissue paper.

Grandpa spoke up again and called me a great little helper who would be so happy in my new family, which would consist of my father's youngest sister, Peggy, and her husband, Richard. "They have a little one now, Kimmy," Grandpa tossed in, like a baby was a prize. "Won't a sister be fun?"

How could I tell these sweet old people that I had no desire to have a sister or to have fun or to be in the company of more young people?

How could I tell them that I knew they were pulling a fast one on me too?

I had already overheard them bad-mouth Richard during cocktail hour. Grandma called him "a divorced Mormon," which equaled "useless son of a bitch" to a devoted Catholic woman like Grandma. Grandpa had said he was "steamed" at Peggy for marrying Richard before she had finished college. They had both refused to talk to their youngest daughter for the better part of a year after she had gone against their wishes with the good-for-nothing Richard.

I knew I could not say anything to change the situation or their minds. Who was I? I was a child. Eleven years old. Nothing.

Instead, I hung my head and just cried. All my plans were about to change—again.

TEN

In Stead

EVEN UNDER THE BEST of circumstances, it is difficult to be a mother. No matter how wondrous my own children were—my Spencer and my Josephine—there have been many dark nights and confused days. When Spencer was little, needing to be close and yet possessing a busy quality that had him wrestle me more than he cuddled me, I was tired. Sleep deprivation lasted almost five years. Nights of unbroken sleep had vanished and as a result, I was crabby and short tempered. A permanent furrow worked itself between my brows creating a nearly constant expression of exhaustion, worry, and self-doubt. For many years, Spencer had a full-time view into this face of distress.

The laundry list of motherhood challenges included breasts that would not cooperate with the mandated rule of nursing, frustration over the lack of privacy and solitude, and the loss of my identity as a career woman, which was then replaced by the lowly position of being a housekeeper, diaper changer, park squatter, and swing pusher.

For a long time—even as I attempted to press these feelings down—a part of me also resented the neediness of the children. Why couldn't they just grow up, keep themselves and their rooms tidy, and get jobs to help support themselves?

Having come from my own childhood, where there had been no evidence of childishness, I was restless with the slow, agonizingly slow, process of getting on with it. What was this need within Spencer to stop and examine the bark of a tree for an hour? How could any child be fascinated, for several weeks, with the opening and closing of the lid on a Fisher Price CD player? What about this throwing himself down, in a busy coffee shop, and screaming at the top of his lungs while pummeling the floor with his fists?

And Jo? How did I, this dark and intense soul, have such a light little girl who found endless delight with flowers, who gathered dolls in groups and talked to them in a language no one could understand, and who needed—no, insisted—on wearing every single princess dress she owned and changed her name from Jo to Belle for a full year?

My kids were just so . . . childlike.

Their very nature was perplexing to me. Vexing at times.

And more, I was plagued with a sense that I, due to my own dark past and resulting cynicism, would deprive them of that natural joy of being unbound, innocent, and free. How could I be a guide for such creatures as my own children? How could I turn off my own impatience and be as present to the joys of life as they were? How could I be the mother they needed instead of the person I was?

When I moved from Grandma and Grandpa's trailer—when I came out of retirement—I found myself in a community called Stead.

"I'm in Stead," I'd say to myself just to hear the word come out of my mouth. Stead. I'm in-stead. I couldn't say it enough. "I'm here now, instead of there." In Stead, instead of being retired. I'm in Stead instead of living with Deb. I'm in Stead instead of being dead, which became a mantra sputtered from the mouths of the aunt and uncle who took me in. "If it wasn't for us, you'd be dead in a gutter somewhere in L.A."

They felt I was lucky to be in Stead.

AUNT PEGGY WAS almost petite compared to Auntie Carol, but her body wasn't small, it was sturdy. With wide shoulders, wide hips, and an ample bosom, Peggy could have filled in Wonder Woman's suit quite nicely. She was solid but womanly.

Peggy was twenty-six years old and a housewife who stayed home with her one-year-old, Kimmy—a sweet, chubby, angelic child with curls of blond hair and huge blue eyes. Peggy passed her time doing laundry, shopping for groceries, and planning meals. At the end of each day, she prepared dinner for Richard—tacos, enchiladas, Salisbury steak, chicken-fried steak, and something called rigatoni, which was mashed-up beef stuffed into pasta shells.

Richard was twenty-eight years old and born on September 19, which seemed to be an odd coincidence. How was it that I ended up in the home of a man who shared Bryan's birthday and the day my mother died? I couldn't fathom it.

RICHARD WAS A tall man with long arms and an oddly shaped torso. With no waist and nearly no behind, his pants slid down his narrow hips and hung midcrack. He was forever tugging them up in a distracted, habitual way. He worked as an appliance repairman, and at the end of the day his fingernails were black with the grease of his profession.

After dinner, most nights, Richard had a ritual where he would turn on the TV, root himself into the sofa and watch episodes of *Bonanza* and *Wild, Wild West*. All the while, he would carve grime from under his nails with a pair of clippers. He did the same to his feet, bending his leg wide around his belly in an act of contortion that seemed physically impossible. Toe jamb.

And Richard smoked. Chain smoker—one after another—all day, all night (until sleep finally made his mouth go slack). When he spoke to me, it was usually to command that I replenish his dwindling supply of smokes, locate his lighter, or empty his overflowing ashtray.

He'd call out, "Hey, no-neck, get me a pack of cigarettes"; "Hey, no-neck, get me my lighter"; "Hey, no-neck, clean out this damn ashtray."

RICHARD WAS ONE of five children who came from what he would call "mountain people," meaning hillbillies who (man and woman alike) chewed tobacco, threw back moonshine, grew their own marijuana, and unloaded ammo on empty beer cans shot from rough rail fences.

Mountain children were raised being called "no-necks."

Children were "hands," not people; they were like pesky livestock, best corralled, contained, and trained to do tough homesteading work.

Richard had had a brutal childhood. He had been whipped more times than he could count. He was proud to have endured—without a whimper—those bloodied beatings. He had gone hungry. He had tasted fear many times.

Richard felt my past was a holiday in Hawaii compared to his childhood and wanted to teach me the lessons of life that I hadn't yet learned. He went to work on me immediately.

LATER I LEARNED that Richard was not only born on September 19th, he was also born in the year 1945. An investigation revealed that Richard shared both birthday and birth year with my birth father—Bill Wright—the man so eager to give me his name when the story began.

First Bryan was born on September 19, then Janet died on that day, then came Richard with that day as his birthday, and finally I was able to connect all of this to my own birth father—exact day and year.

There was no explanation for the synchronicity. The information, once revealed, made me feel as if I teetered on the edge of cosmic complexity beyond my capacity for comprehension.

While Richard seemed an impossible match as my father, he was an exact replica. Had I attracted him to me? Was there something unique in my chemistry that energetically vibrated with a character like Richard and if yes, why and how?

It seemed so odd that life gave me a father (Bill) and then took him away, gave me another father (Bud) and took him away too, and then, gave me Richard. Richard instead of Bill. Richard instead of Bud.

RICHARD AND PEGGY's house was one level with three bedrooms and asbestos siding. A chainlink fence surrounded the yard and the grass was burned brown.

I was given a place to sleep in the sewing room at the back of the house and Peggy enrolled me in school, a big challenge due to the fact that few records were available.

I told her I had lived alone at the commune and dropped out of school but Peggy did not believe me. She made calls over the course of many days but found nothing. I tried to tell her, one more time, how I had only done a smattering of education—here and there. Again, Peggy rolled her eyes. She said I knew how to read and write. That kind of thing didn't come from magic. There was no use in telling Peggy I taught myself to read and write. She wasn't much for paying attention.

After taking some tests to place me in sixth grade, a full year behind kids my own age, Peggy and Richard became my legal guardians. In a few weeks, my bedroom set arrived from L.A. Deb had sent it.

My new life in Stead began.

ELEVEN

THE LITTLE BOAT

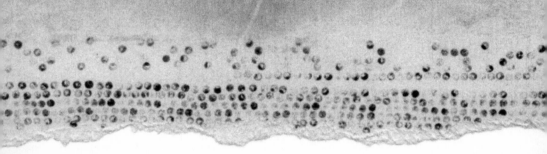

WHEN A HOLIDAY came around the calendar—Labor Day, Memorial Day, Fourth of July—Peggy and Richard cut themselves out of Stead and set up an exact duplicate of their life in the woods. They brought their trailer, a cook stove, coolers of food, packs of cigarettes, and pots for making coffee. Kimmy came too and with her came all her baby stuff: playpen, diapers, high chair, and toys. The only thing they left behind was the TV.

IT WAS LABOR Day and we were out in the woods. Richard was wedged in a fold-up chair, his foot near his nose. The canvas of the chair strained against his bulk and he carved at his big toe with his pocketknife. Kimmy was down for a nap. Peggy played solitaire at the picnic table.

There was nothing for me to clean or cook. The campsite was all picked up. And for a change, they weren't bossing me around to get cigarettes or make a pot of coffee.

I pushed my hands into the pockets of my shorts and wandered toward the creek.

Richard called out, "Don't go far."

"All right," I said.

I had adapted by doing what I was told, keeping my mouth shut, and just getting along. For the most part, it wasn't so bad and Peggy was kind to Kimmy. I admired her for that.

A few feet down the trail, I spotted a pinecone the size of a football. I kicked it with the side of my foot and it rolled a few feet ahead. I caught up to the pinecone and kicked it again—harder this time— and it splashed into the creek.

The forest smelled like pine and earth and things that grew and died all at the same time. The ponderosa pine trees stood tall and solid and their high branches held firm to a bounty of pinecones and long needles.

ABOUT THREE MONTHS earlier, at the end of sixth grade, Peggy sent me on a trip to San Francisco to visit a distant cousin I didn't know. The woman had a little girl, maybe seven years old, and I got the feeling that maybe, just maybe, I was being sent away—or perhaps the trip was a little test to see if another family would take me. I'm sure, given the right situation, Richard and Peggy would have passed the responsibility of raising me to someone else— like tired runners eager to pass off the baton. I was like a package no one had sent for. At least with Bud and Janet, they *wanted* a little girl. But Peggy and Richard? I sensed that the primary incentive for my presence in their home was as domestic help and there was a pretty good chunk of change that came in my name. My Social Security and Veteran's Administration benefits added up to a third of Richard's earnings.

Before being sent to San Francisco, I questioned Peggy about the trip—the why and the what—but Richard yelled, "It's none of your damn business why you are going. Just do what you are told."

I WENT TO San Francisco, stayed a few days, and in the night my cousin's boyfriend crawled into my bed.

It wasn't intercourse but he did things a grown man had no business doing to a little girl. When I tried to get away, he pinned me down and told me to enjoy it. "You know you want it," he said. "Come on baby, relax."

Enjoy what?

I told my cousin what her boyfriend had done and she sent me back to Stead. My cousin told me not to tell but I wasn't loyal to her. I told Peggy and Richard right away.

Richard said I was lying and Peggy just rolled her eyes. They both said I was quite a little storyteller.

I was blunt. I was full of questions. I had a way of talking about things no one else wanted to talk about—but frankly I remember a lesson from when I lived with Janet. She told me, "Just don't lie, Jenny. Lying is like a trap and you always get caught." Her words stuck with me, that and the fact that she told me that if I ever did lie, she'd wash my mouth with soap.

Fear and some good common sense were enough to sway me off the liar's path.

But Richard and Peggy—perhaps because they were accustomed to being dishonest—were suspect of me as well, in the same way Peggy did not believe my story about missing school and learning to read. Richard did not believe this story. They had no idea that I had also been raped before—at a summer camp while living with Deb and that there had been another molestation when I was six.

If I *wanted* to lie, I would have conjured a really good one about rescuing kittens from drowning or helping an old lady across the road. My foundational identity was to be a divine hero. I would not, under any circumstances, lie about something as nasty as a man messing between my legs. "Why?" I wanted to scream at them. "Why would I lie about this?"

THE PINECONE BOBBED down the fast-moving creek and I kneeled on the soft edge of the bank. I plunged my hands into the icy clear water and dug my fingers into the soft creek bed just to feel the sand and mud and rocks. I pulled up a few stones and they were smooth and round, worn that way by being in the creek. I built a little stack of the rocks, the way you do to mark your way on a hiking path. The stacks of stones said, "I was here," in case anyone wanted to know.

A wedge of driftwood floated past and it was wide at one side and narrow at the other.

I forgot the rocks and snagged the driftwood. I turned the wood this way and that and it was shaped almost like a boat with a rudder.

At my back, Richard was still crouched over his foot and Peggy dealt herself a new hand.

I got an idea.

I went up the dirt path that ran along the creek and climbed a small rise. At the top was a still pool and I released the driftwood. I jogged downstream again.

In a few minutes, the driftwood floated down and the top was still dry, even after its journey. I decided it *was* a boat. I went back up the trail with the little boat in my hand and on the way, picked a few wild flowers. I laid the flowers on the flat surface of the boat and released it once more.

The boat bobbed on the current, safe and sound. "Such a good boat," I said to the wood, not realizing I was talking out loud.

I added some pine needles, a rock, and a leaf and did the same trek up the side of the creek.

Up and down I went. I don't even know how many times. It was that little hunk of wood, water, and sun. It was good. I felt happy in a way that was unfamiliar to me.

Eventually, inevitably, I named my boat.

I called it Catherine and felt so proud of myself for coming up with such a good name, all on my own. I said it over and over again—chattering to myself—*Catherine, Catherine, Catherine.*

WHEN WE WERE done camping and driving home, I sat in the back seat of the car and looked out the side window. Packing to leave a campsite was one thing after another—Richard yelled and Peggy bossed. He called me "no-neck" and "good for nothing." She rolled her eyes and sighed a lot. Between the two of them, it was like being in a blender. My nerves were shot.

Richard and Peggy were up front and Kimmy was on Peggy's lap, asleep or on her way to sleep. She sucked her thumb—content.

Afternoon sun split light through the forest, making sideways streamers, and that's when I realized that I had left Catherine at the side of the creek.

I patted at my pockets to make sure and yes, it was true. I had left my boat.

I put my hand over my mouth but not before I said, "Oh my god," out loud.

Peggy jumped a little and twisted her head around to look back at me.

"What?"

I almost said, "I left my driftwood boat at the side of the creek," but I didn't. It sounded so stupid. Peggy was never going to understand. Richard would say something mean.

I started to cry instead, with gulping, hiccupping sobs that made it one hundred percent clear I was a bigger baby than Kimmy.

"What's the matter?" Peggy asked.

I shook my head since there was no way I could talk.

Richard adjusted the mirror to look back at me. "Shut up already," he said. "You're going to wake Kimmy."

"Richard, enough," Peggy said, and when she spoke like that

he would actually do what she said. She reached over the seat and touched my knee. "Are you hurt?"

I shook my head to say no and swiped at my drippy nose with the back of my arm. I looked out the window like changing my view might help me stop crying but then I just thought about Catherine again and how she was at the side of the creek, alone in the dark. I could see her in my mind, surrounded by leaves and daisies and rocks. She had been my boat. My good, sturdy, wonderful boat, with the best name in the world, but I had left her. I had abandoned her.

Richard finally said I had better shut up or he was going to give me something to really cry about.

I wanted to tell him to go ahead and hit me because, frankly, a blow from him would have been a merciful relief from the way it felt to know Catherine was back there, alone in the dark.

WHEN WE GOT home, I went to my room and closed the door. At my desk, I pulled out a sheet of paper and wrote: *All time favorite girls name: Catherine.* I put the sheet of paper into my *Columbia Viking Desk Encyclopedia* under the letter C, so I'd never forget.

TWELVE

FREE WILL

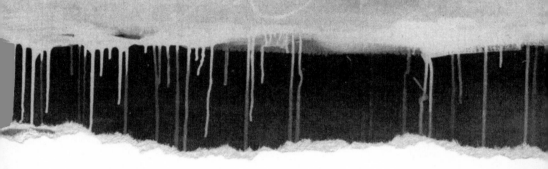

MY CHILDREN WILL TELL YOU many things about me—they will say I have been sad, I have been frustrated, I have been confused and even full of doubt about the right way to parent them—but they will never tell you I have silenced their dreams or stifled their full expressions of curiosity, sorrow, frustration, anger, confusion, or joy.

Josephine needed to change her name to Belle for a year. Okay.

I'd say, "It's your world, girlfriend," and did my best to call her Belle until she was ready to be Jo again. She also had a phase where she wanted to wear every pair of pants, every pair of underwear, and every princess dress to preschool. Okay. "It's your world," I'd say while wondering if the child had been a refugee in a past life.

When Spencer needed to dance in the kitchen, doing an imitation of John Travolta—that was fine. When he wanted to do Tae Kwan Do, learn the drums, take up rollerblading—okay, okay, okay.

He wanted to read Japanese comic books, study Japanese animation, and eat sushi every day. Okay. Okay. Okay.

These children of mine are not mine. They are themselves. I just kept them as safe as I knew how and said, "It's your world."

If expression, a full wide range of self-expression is all I give to my own children—as a result of my own childhood—I consider the adventure of motherhood to be my greatest success. And if that is what I was being taught by the experiences I endured, then I can say I learned. Oh yes, I learned.

IT WAS ANOTHER day in Stead. I rode the bus, went to school, fell asleep on my desk, rode the bus back to the house, and walked into the front door.

Peggy was watching *Donahue* while she folded laundry.

"How was school?" she asked, looking up from her task.

"Fine."

Kimmy sat on the floor, surrounded by Tupperware containers in shades of pastel. She popped up, containers rolling in every direction, and toddled over to the front door. Like I was a moving object she needed to catch, Kimmy lunged at my legs and squeezed hard.

Kimmy was always happy to see me. She was the same with Peggy, Richard, Grandma, Grandpa, and the mailman. Kimmy loved the world.

I shoved the door closed with my hip, careful not to knock Kimmy over.

"Hi, Kimmy, hi, hi," I said. I made my voice bright and happy, being nice to Kimmy because she deserved kindness. "Let me go now, Sweetie. Let Jenny go."

Kimmy opened her arms and grinned up at me like a happy fool. I wanted to tell her to wise up and stop liking me but I figured she'd get the hang of it soon enough.

"Why don't you put that stuff into your room and come help me," Peggy said. "I need to talk to you."

"Okay," I said.

I carried my schoolbooks into my room and Kimmy followed like a pup. On my pillow, was a slip of unfamiliar paper.

"Ba ba?" Kimmy pointed at a stuffed lamb also on the bed and I nudged the lamb her way.

"Baby," she said, grabbing it with both hands. Kimmy hugged the stuffed animal as if it were the most important toy on the planet.

The page had an official-looking blue seal and read Non-Identifying Information. Further down it read, "Mother," and there were details: blond hair, blue eyes, fair complexion.

My eyes went out of focus and I swayed a little.

I went back to the living room and Kimmy followed.

"What's this?"

Peggy did a fast glance over her shoulder. "Oh, that was in Bud's legal papers." She waved her hand like it was nothing. "I finally got around to sorting that stuff out."

I felt like I was rising out of my skin and away. I was smoke, mist, wind.

"Is this what you wanted to talk about?" I heard myself ask.

"Huh?"

I waved the page at Peggy. "This paper? Is this what you wanted to talk about?"

Peggy shook her head. "No, no, I thought you'd want it, that's all."

Kimmy held the stuffed animal up for Peggy's inspection.

"Oh, Sweetie, you have a new baby," Peggy said. "Did Jenny let you have that?"

Kimmy lifted her huge blue eyes as if to ask the question and I nodded.

"Baby," Kimmy cooed.

"That's so nice," Peggy said. She went back to folding and watching her program. Kimmy dropped to the floor with the lamb. She shoved the stuffed animal into a bowl—trying to make it fit.

ONE TIME, AT the grocery store, Kimmy got lost. She had been toddling next to Peggy and wandered away while Peggy looked at the ingredient list on a box of Hamburger Helper.

"Well, let me tell you, my heart just sank into my shoes," Peggy said, her hand clutching her chest.

Kimmy had made her way over to the produce section, all alone and then started to cry.

The manager of the store, bag boys, checkout girls, and other shoppers were all frantic trying to help Kimmy but she couldn't talk.

Peggy was at the other end of the store, going crazy too. She was crying as she searched through the cereal aisle, the dairy section, and the bakery.

Kimmy wasn't lost for more than ten minutes but those ten minutes were so hard on Kimmy, she almost passed out and Peggy was sick for the rest of the day. Mother and child separated created trauma in both of them.

I WENT BACK to my room and this time, Kimmy didn't follow.

Sitting down on the edge of my bed, I read out loud: "Mother: 17, blond hair, blue eyes, 5' 8.5", 128 pounds, English, Scottish, German, and Irish ancestry. Father: 17, brunette, brown eyes, olive complexion, 5' 11", 160 pounds, German and Irish ancestry."

I waited and waited, as if I had just spoken some magic formula and now my true parents would appear. Nothing.

I read the page again.

Mother, father, German, Irish, 5' 8.5", 5' 11", blond, brunette.

My hands, arms, and body got very cold from the shock of memory or perhaps the tripped wire of amnesia.

All I could think to do was to fold the sheet of paper in half, in half again, and then in half one more time as if to make the information as small as I was becoming in my own mind and I whirled back to the beginning when I had been separated from my mother.

I put the page into my *Columbia Viking Desk Encyclopedia*, right next to the sheet that read, *Catherine: All time favorite girls name*, and then I crawled into bed.

"HEY! WHAT ARE you doing?" Peggy bellowed. The doorway framed her solid body. "Are you asleep?"

I sat up in bed and the covers fell away.

"It's not bedtime," she said. "What in the world is wrong with you? Get up!"

Peggy retreated down the hall, talking to herself. "Geez Louise. I need help with dinner. Richard will be home soon."

A slash of light from the overhead in the hall cut into my room. The smell of ground beef hung in the air.

My mind was tied to the sheet of paper folded away in my encyclopedia. Was it still there? Had it been real?

I felt as if I existed in two places—the displaced alternative Jennifer who adapted to exist in Richard and Peggy's world and the original baby born to the strangers detailed on that small bit of paper.

Rather than examine the sheet again, I stumbled out of bed and into the kitchen.

Kimmy sat in her froggy high chair, bits of cheese, cheerios, and olives were scattered over her tray as snacks.

Peggy jostled past, making a big deal of gathering a brick of cheese, a head of lettuce, and a bag of tomatoes from the refrigerator shelf. "Oh my god, we have so much to do. Cut up these tomatoes, then grate the cheese. Come on, chop, chop. Richard will be here any minute."

Peggy always got into a fever before Richard came home, as if her value was tied to making a meal and having it on the table at the moment he walked in the door.

She stomped to the stove and used a spatula to push around the ground beef in the pan.

I picked up a knife and a tomato and this brought more rage. "Oh my god, don't cut before you wash your hands! You know better."

Kimmy shoved a Cheerio into her mouth, blue eyes wide in the way of small children. Silent witnesses, omniscient observers, pure beings of awareness. She was perfect presence in the room.

"Oh, right," I said.

I turned on the faucet, washed my hands with soap, and rinsed the bubbles off. There was comfort in the heat of the water.

"Now you're here," Peggy said, "what I *wanted* to talk to you about—before Richard got home—is that we have decided to adopt you."

I turned off the water and looked at my aunt.

"Adopt me?"

"That's right," Peggy said.

Smiling, she took two cans of refried beans from the cabinet and opened each one with the electric can opener. Her voice mixed with the grinding sound of the machine and she said they were tired of explaining who I was and how I came to live with them. She said if I had the same name, it would be so much easier on everyone. I could have a fresh start too—put my past behind me, and since we all looked so much alike, no one would ever have to know they weren't my true parents. The grind of the electric can opener stopped and Peggy turned over the coagulated beans into a silver saucepan. "Isn't that great?" she asked. "I think it's great. Richard thinks it's great."

I gripped the counter. In the sink there were bits of onion peel and an empty Styrofoam wrapper from the ground beef. The bottom of the Styrofoam container was coated with cow blood. I thought I might throw up.

"Would you cut up tomatoes already," Peggy said. "Come on now, chop, chop. "

Like a robot, I cut through the tomato, making the round fruit into a pulp of small red squares and finally found my voice.

"What about Bryan? Are you adopting him too?"

Peggy shook the pan of meat on the burner.

"Well, no, of course not. You know very well he's with Uncle Larry in Oklahoma now. He has his own family."

"But he *is* my family. He's my brother."

"Honestly, Jenny," Peggy said. "You know you two don't get along. Why are you talking about Bryan now?"

"I don't know," I said. "Can I be adopted when I have a brother out there?"

"Well, of course you can," she said, laughing as if what I said was lunacy.

I wanted to ask if Uncle Larry was adopting Bryan but I didn't. I backed my own mind up, like an old truck grinding through rusted gears. I searched through what she had said. They were both adopting me. Richard too.

"Uncle Richard wants to adopt me?"

"Well, of course he does. Richard loves you. We all do."

Now I was certain I was going to be sick. I looked hard at Peggy—almost angry.

"*You* love me?" I asked.

Peggy turned from the stove and looked at me with her mouth open.

"Well, of course we do," she said, indignant. Color lifted on her cheeks. "My goodness, you've been here for more than a year now. We've opened our home to you and have shared our lives. If that is not love, I don't know what is."

Peggy stood there with her fists on her hips and her spatula dripped grease on the floor. She believed what she was saying. She was utterly convinced that her decision to adopt was the right one for the family and for me. I could not speak. There wasn't room for my voice in her version of reality. I did not exist.

A FEW MONTHS later, the adoption plan ripened to fullness.

Richard and Peggy took me to a courthouse in Reno. I stood before a judge and they stood on either side of me.

The judge asked if I agreed to this adoption of my own free will. He had to ask it again because I didn't hear him the first time.

Everyone in court looked at me. The judge, a lady who sat over at a little type machine, Richard, Peggy, and a bunch of other people. Strangers.

In my head was a voice that wanted to ask the judge if he could define "free will." I wanted to see if his definition would line up with what I knew the words to mean.

Richard pushed his arm against my shoulder and looked at me

like I better answer the man or I was going to get smacked up the back of my head.

I blurted out, "I do."

Laughter erupted in the courtroom. Richard snickered. And the judge hit his gavel with a crack—like rock hitting rock.

In that sound, Jennifer Caste Lauck became Jenny Duemore. I had been erased.

THIRTEEN

THREE THINGS SHE DOESN'T KNOW

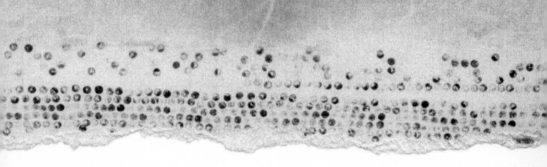

She is wickedly smart.

She is hysterically funny.

She is fantastically gorgeous.

Not necessarily in that order.

And yes, there is even more—good things, every single one—but she won't allow herself to consider herself in such grand terms. If she thinks of herself with any kind of praise, a feeling of itching anxiety sends her running to organize a drawer, fold laundry, wash the floor on her hands and knees, or clean out the refrigerator. As she fritters over these meaningless tasks of order, she fills her head—like a countermeasure—with all that's flawed. *You talk too loud, your rear end is too big, your nose—what a honker on your face, and you're not really that smart, no, you're just street smart. You're scrappy.*

The voice in her head is a combination of the voices she's heard throughout her life: Richard, Peggy, Deb, Auntie Carol. And the voice is also unique. It is her own.

The voice is like a form of protection—a firm taskmaster that needs her to lay low. It tells her she will die if she brings attention to herself. The voice believes that to know her merits is dangerous. Such knowledge would put her one step away from becoming arrogant or proud and both of these very human qualities would then lead to her standing out in the crowd. To be outstanding would bring attention, and to bring attention would make her a clear target. The voice tells her she is most safe when she is below the horizon line and behind the scenes. When she tidies up, helps without complaint, and follows the rules, all is well for her. Anything else, any large expression, is disaster.

This is how she makes it as Richard and Peggy's daughter—Jenny Duemore.

On the surface.

But deep below the surface of herself, there lives another truth. It is a seed, awaiting the mysterious conditions necessary for a new self to emerge. One day, those conditions will exist and the voice in her head will stop ordering her to drop down low and she will rise from her hiding place, scramble over the edge, and stand to her full and glorious height. She will dust the dirt of the past off her shoulders and legs and then, she will take flight. A phoenix rising won't be her metaphor. Such a suggestion will be too puny and passé.

She will be without a name, an awe-inspiring sight, and will rise as bright as the sun. Right away, in one blink, she will merge into that light.

Most won't see the ascension of the small human who once lay so low. When people finally look, trying to see this magnificent sight, she will be no more than a speck in the forever blue sky.

FOURTEEN

One Thing I Do Know

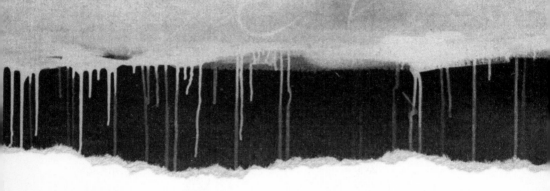

"I'm going to college."

Despite the nullifications of being made into a Duemore—I was firm in my belief that had been implanted by my father. "Go to college, Jenny," he had told me. "Education is freedom. Go to college. It's important."

Did Bud actually say these words or was this conviction contained in my cells? It's hard to know. Memory is so cagey and also such a prison. I can only say there is evidence in a file at the VA. Apparently, a man—just prior to my being adopted—had interviewed me. I have the fuzziest memory of him in the living room of Richard and Peggy's house just before the adoption day.

"What do you plan to do when you grow up, little girl?" he asked. A clipboard was balanced on his lap.

"I'm going to college, sir," I said.

I remember the man laughing and writing these words down. He wrote, "This child is quite adamant about her higher education and her guardian and aunt has agreed to save all benefits received for said higher education."

RICHARD AND PEGGY moved five times over the six years we coexisted as a family.

Moving from Stead, we lived in the city of Reno. Next, we went to a double-wide mobile home on the outskirts of Reno, and then moved to an apartment in a damp Washington town called Longview. In Longview, Richard, Peggy, and Kimmy stayed together and I was packed off to live with Richard's younger brother, Irv.

Irv had a young wife named Dede and they had two big hound dogs—Duke and Earl. Irv, Dede, Duke, and Earl were all wedged into a single-wide mobile trailer in a tiny town called Toutle, which was little more than a few paved streets, a scramble of wild blackberry bushes, and acres of pine trees. There was a river, the Toutle River, and it ran down from Mt. Saint Helens. It rained so often and was so humid that mold grew on mold.

For one school term, I jammed into their tight, damp world. During the day I went to school and at night slept on a fold-out sofa in the minuscule living room.

Every night, Duke and Earl took mountain-sized shits and pissed rivers of bitter urine on the floor around my bed. Every morning, I woke to Irv skidding, barefooted, through the mess while he said, "Shit, goddamn, piss."

Richard, Peggy, Kimmy, and me finally regathered and settled, for a few years, in a mouse-and-rat infested house at the end of a road called Morton in a town called Winlock. Richard worked fixing appliances. Peggy stayed home with Kimmy. And I went to Mt. Saint Helen's High.

Winlock locals were—for the most part—farmers, laborers, and housewives. The average education in the area was a high school diploma. After that, most kids went to work for their parents, joined the military, and/or got married and had babies.

People expected very little of themselves in our new town. Ambition, beyond winning a football game, was remarkably low. Accordingly, very little was expected of me. Under these conditions, I flourished.

I joined the French Club, played basketball (both junior varsity and varsity at the same time), became captain of the junior varsity team, and wrote a bit for the student newspaper. I was voted the Funniest Girl.

By the time I reached my freshman year, I was a dervish of accomplishment who, for money, baby-sat and took a summer job waiting tables at a take-out place on Interstate 90. The truckers, stopping over for coffee and plate-sized cinnamon rolls would tell me I was pretty. They gave over fat tips.

It was at this restaurant that one of the truckers told me I looked a lot like a guy he knew. He said, "Hey, you look just like a guy who lives just south of Seattle—Renton, I think. Name of Wright. I swear you could be his kid."

I was fifteen years old.

I put the pot of coffee on the counter and looked hard at that man, that trucker, and said, "I was adopted as a baby."

The trucker nodded like he knew this. He seemed unfazed—as if lost children were a part of his every day. He told me he would ask around. He left me a ten-dollar tip, a lot of money back then. I never saw that trucker again.

JUST UP THE road from that diner, my birth father Bill did live in Renton, Washington, and later moved even closer, to a town called Yelm. He was with a woman named Helen. They had a son named Tom. I didn't know all this about my birth father for many years—it all came out long after I was done pouring coffee.

MIDYEAR, WHEN I was a sophomore, we moved away from Winlock and went further east—to Spokane.

Richard was told he had strong people skills and was provided managerial training to run the service department of a store in Spokane.

When this bit of good fortune happened, I was sixteen years old—twenty-four months from sweet liberation.

I was very unhappy to leave Winlock behind but my feelings were not considered in the decision to move.

In Spokane, I entered Mead Senior High and promptly joined the drill team—where again, I was voted the funniest girl. In typing class, I got myself up to sixty words a minute, error free, and this skill helped secure employment. I worked half of each school day as a secretary for a real estate company.

Another accomplishment was my placement in an Honors English class, which was the result of state testing that showed I had strong scores in reading and writing.

In the midst of my year in Honors English, I was pulled aside by the teacher, Ms. Carla Nuxoll, who dressed in flowing garments and was a slight woman with a 'fro of light brown hair—kinked tight of its own accord.

Ms. Nuxoll held one of my compositions and told me I was a fine writer. "A truly fine writer," she insisted. "Where did you learn to write like this?"

Unnerved by her proximity and suspicious of adults in general, I could only stare at her hair and the way it caught the light and shined rainbow colors through the separate filaments. Something about her reminded me of that time, in the communal house, when I watched those babies being born.

"I dunno," I mumbled.

Ms. Nuxoll regarded me for a long time, a furrow working between her eyebrows as if I were a riddle on a crossword.

"Well," she finally said, straightening her shoulders and lifting her proud chin. "You must consider being a writer as a profession. You are that talented."

Her statement caught my attention and pulled me to my own full height.

"Can I make money as a writer?" I asked.

"Certainly," she said.

"How?"

"As a journalist," she said, "in the short term and then a novelist perhaps. Or short stories."

In my head, a series of computations were being run. *Be a writer. Make money. Escape.* I had a plan.

AND THEN EVERYTHING went horribly wrong.

Richard was fired, something about the black market sale of out-of-warranty appliances. He said he was framed. The whole thing was a scam. It was politics.

Richard was then home, all day, everyday. He watched TV and made a nuisance of himself. I knew because it was my job to fix the meals, do laundry, clean the house, and care for Kimmy. Richard followed me around, bossy and rude, saying, "You're doing a half-assed job, you no-neck brat. Get out there and wash my truck, vacuum the living room again, blah, blah, blah."

He drank brandy in his coffee.

He slept on the sofa in the afternoon.

He was depressed.

Peggy was the one to support the family. She became embittered by their reversal of roles.

This was about the time they both began to push me to join the military rather than go to college. Peggy made enlistment sound like a Parisian holiday. "You can travel," she said, "and they pay for college."

Graduation was one year away.

I WAS SO damn busy with school, my job, my homework, all my domestic responsibilities, and my extracurricular activities, but still, somehow, I found time to become obsessed with the notion of sex.

As if a time bomb had exploded inside my seventeen-year-old body, I was on fire with a desire to have intercourse.

If one traced my secret history, the explanation was there in the annals of time. My own mother had had sex when she was sixteen, and look at the shame, the concealment, the denial, and the forgotten result (which was me). Full of wild adolescent hormones, I was burning to explode from my faux skin and enter into truth no matter the cost. A sexual encounter could be a doorway to freedom.

I was quick to choose an object of adoration—a new boy who had moved in across the street. Dark and mysterious, this new boy played the saxophone and was painfully shy. He called himself a military brat—his father was in the air force. He was perfect for me—moody, emotionally unavailable, and withdrawn. The fact that he showed no interest in me for months, even though we lived across the street from each other, made him that much more of a catch.

I charmed, smiled, and seduced him with relentless focus. Once he noticed me, I made it clear that I would "put out" for the right guy. What boy, at seventeen, doesn't want to get laid?

After school and in secret, I got myself on the pill, because I was not—under any circumstances—getting pregnant.

And then we did it!

Sex.

Total disaster.

The boy across the street was a novice, of course. Most virgins are. And I was a ticking time bomb of repressed sexual abuse. Our experimental and very painful copulation made me cry so hard that the kid was paralyzed by confusion and could not get through the process of inserting tab A into slot B. I urged him forward, all the while reassuring him that all girls cried from the ecstasy. Didn't he know? Crying was in all the books, I said with worldly confidence, between sobs and sniffs. When we were finally done with the wretched act and he scurried away, I stopped being stoic and let the tears rain. The physical pain was bad, but worse, there was so much inside of me that was hidden and buried and yet alive in my cells. I had blundered into the dark realms and hidden corridors of myself but had no way to understand where I had landed. There were no therapists, no teachers, no guides, and no wise women in my life. I had only my books and my own mind, which was full of insane ideas including one that said, *Now you've done it. You've had sex and are no longer a virgin. Major sin!*

The time I once used to lure the boy across the street was redirected to time served at the Catholic Church where Peggy and Richard sometimes took mass on Christmas Eve and Easter.

On my own, I went to confession, did thousands of Our Father and Hail Mary prayers on a ten-cent rosary, and prostrated myself in front of the statue of St. Mary Magdalene. Since she was considered the whore of the bunch during biblical times, I begged Mary for divine insight and wisdom. We were two women with a common bond. If she became a saint, in her fallen state, surely my actions were redeemable too.

I have to wonder if I was prostrating myself for my own sins, which were pretty benign considering the outcome, or was I actually reliving the shame absorbed by my mother in 1963 and thus absorbed by me as the baby she carried? Was I trying to heal the both of us through my reenactment of her past? Was I, in fact, healing us, in some way, due to my clear-headed decision to take the pill and avoid an untimely pregnancy?

In 1981, Ronald Reagan was president and, with the aid of Congress, cut off Social Security death benefits for all students who were not full-time college students as of March 1982.

Peggy took me to a restaurant called The Village Inn to tell me this news. She was panicked and wanted me to drop out of high school in order to get into college six months ahead of schedule.

"It's the only way to keep your benefits," she said.

Peggy wore a white and black polka-dot blouse—rayon—that tied at her neck. Under her chin was an enormous bow. Over this top, she wore a cheap gray blazer and a matching wool skirt.

Richard was with us too. Upon Peggy's urging, he had been interviewing for jobs. He wore a corduroy sports jacket two sizes too small and hunched over a plate of home fries, elbows splayed on each side of the plate. His cigarette burned in the ashtray on the table and the air was laced with his smoke.

Leave high school early? Get into college now? No. I was just filling out all the applications. No, no, no.

In my most professional, secretarial tone of voice, newly

acquired from answering phones at my real estate office job, I said it was okay to let the benefits slide. "After all, you've been saving all these years so I'll have enough for school."

Richard steered a glance at Peggy, at me, and then at Peggy again, but Peggy only stared into her cup of coffee.

"There ain't no money saved for you," Richard drawled.

"Yes," I said, "there is." I leaned closer to Peggy, as if we were the only ones at the table. "Don't you remember?"

Red stains lifted on Peggy's cheeks and swept down her neck.

"That's a goddamned lie!" Richard said.

He hit the table and the dishes jumped against each other. People gawked. The waitress, coming over to refill Peggy's coffee, changed course.

"No," I said. I put my hand on Peggy's wrist, so she'd look at me. "You said. You promised."

"Now listen to me you snot-nosed kid—" Richard started.

I held up my hand to stop him—a move I had seen Peggy do several times when she had had enough. Miraculously, he shut his mouth.

I willed Peggy to look at me, eye to eye, woman to woman, and finally she lifted her chin. She glanced at Richard, just for a moment and then cleared her throat.

"You must have misunderstood me," she said. "There's no money saved for college."

Was it the expression on my face—the shock—or was it just the way he was? I'm sure I heard Richard laugh at me. I'm sure I heard him go, "Heh heh heh."

IT'S TOO EASY to hate Richard. It's too easy to hate Peggy, too. I don't hate them. I don't want to hate them.

I do want to understand. I do want the truth. People have a right to these things. I can understand anything, if you just tell me the truth. Had Peggy said, "Geez, Jenny, I'm really sorry but after Richard lost his job we had to spend that college money." Or, "I didn't plan to save that money, not ever, I just said that to the man from the VA in order to look good in front of him." Or, "I screwed up, I made a mistake. I'm sorry. How can I make it up to you?"

None of this was said.

Perhaps it is too much to ask from people who have been so wounded—somewhere in their own pasts—to make things right. Perhaps all I can do is let it go and apply a bit of healing amnesia to this situation. I don't know the answer. Perhaps there is no answer. Perhaps this is just life, which is complicated and unfair and sometimes even cruel. Maybe it has to be this way in order for me to finally and fully appreciate how life is also simple, sweet, and beautiful.

FIFTEEN

SWEET INDEPENDENCE

ON THE DAY I moved out of Richard and Peggy's house, a gust of bitter wind blew over Spokane and then it began to snow. A blanket of white covered the lawns, the streets, and the rooftops. So much snow came down, I felt as if it were a sign. The past was gone and a new start was in front of me.

My feet slipped on the sidewalk as I carried my bookcase to the front door of my new apartment.

Up ahead, in the tumbling and swirling snow, stood a young woman. In the glow of the porch light, she looked like a snow angel.

"Here," she said, stepping forward. "Let me help."

She grabbed the other end of the bookcase and together we went the rest of the way.

"New neighbor?" she asked.

"Yep," I said, "1A."

"2A," she said.

"Nice to meet you, 2A," I said, and this made her laugh.

I shouldered the door open and we carried the bookcase into the living room.

My new place was a one-bedroom apartment near the community college where I was a full-time student. The living room was scattered with boxes and my princess bedroom set.

"Actually, I'm Patty," she said.

Once the bookcase was deposited, I stomped snow off my feet and extended my hand.

"Nice to meet you, Patty," I said.

She was about twenty-five years old and shaking her hand felt like holding a little bird—her bones were so fine. Patty looked around at my meager belongings, a smile fixed to her face.

"Do you have a daughter?"

"What?"

She pointed at the disassembled princess bedroom furniture, scattered between the boxes, and I finally understood. She thought I was a mother!

I laughed so hard, I had to pinch my side. A mother? Me? That was a good one.

At this point—having just left home—motherhood and I were not on good terms. In my wake there had been Peggy, Deb, and Janet—not to mention the mother who left me in the hospital on the day I had been born. Motherhood translated to mean inhumane in my vocabulary. I'd become a giraffe before I'd become a mother— or so I thought as I laughed in front of this stranger.

"No, I don't have a child," I finally said, wiping tears of mirth from the corners of my eyes. "I'm saving this furniture. It's mine. I'm not even married."

"Oh," she said, put off by my borderline hysteria. She crossed her arms and shifted a little from side to side. "I'm getting married," she finally said. Her ring finger held a very impressive rock.

Since marriage was about as interesting as the subject of mothers, I could only muster a tepid response.

"Congratulations," I said. "Very pretty."

Patty did a hop and clapped her little hands as if marriage were a pinnacle of accomplishment.

I squinted as I considered her. She seemed familiar to me.

"Have we ever met before?" I asked.

She shook her head. "I don't think so," she said.

"Huh, you seem very familiar."

"Yeah," Patty agreed. "You too."

FOR THE FIRST month of being on my own, I slept for twelve hours a day.

I wanted to purge Peggy and Richard and all that had been. I didn't want to know them, I didn't want to think about what had passed between us as a so-called family and I didn't want to be their daughter.

I was haunted by the legal fact that they continued to be my parents.

I tried to figure out a way to null and void them but didn't know how such a thing would be possible.

Sleeping was all I could figure out.

"IT'S BEING ADOPTED," Patty said. "That's what we have in common."

"I still can't believe you're adopted too." I said.

"I still can't believe you were adopted twice," she said.

We were in my living room, and she curled in the corner of my new L-shaped sofa. We drank glasses of red wine, which she brought as a housewarming gift. I had all new things. Mature furnishings—a sofa, an end table, a dining set, and drapes.

With glasses of wine, we unfurled the stories of our lives and Patty's tale lifted simple and easy, like wind on a spring day. She grew up in Spokane, went to the same school her whole life, and had a lot of friends. Her adoptive parents loved her and she visited them all the time.

I felt my own story was not even capable of lift off in light of her tale. I didn't tell her much. I was in the process of sealing up the vault of my past. I was like one of those optimistic souls who believed you could contain radioactive waste if you just poured enough concrete, not realizing that it didn't work that way. Like radiation, the past and our shadows are alive.

I just changed the subject.

"How do you like my place?" I asked. "Groovy, huh?"

Patty looked around. "You've done such a nice job," she said.

"It's amazing what you can do with a credit card," I quipped.

She sipped her wine and considered me for a long time. I thought, for sure, she was going to try to pry my history out, but then she said, "I'm searching for my first mother."

She put her glass on the table and looked relieved. "You are the first person I've told."

I put my own glass on the coffee table and pulled my knees to my chest, as if recoiling from her and such a ludicrous plan. Search for her mother?

"Why?" I asked.

"Why am I telling you or why am I searching?"

"Both, I guess."

She looked up at the ceiling, as if to find an answer.

"Well, I just have to search, it's in my heart," she said, "and I felt like you might understand."

"Me?"

"Well, sure," she said.

She looked at me, all starry eyed and hopeful and I wanted to suggest she go live with Peggy for a few months, that would shake her out of her romantic notions about mother. Patty was a woman who desperately needed a reality shakedown. Mothers were bad news.

"Oh," I finally said, "well, good luck with that."

I picked up my wine again and sipped the dark, bitter liquid. Patty did the same.

"Thanks," she said.

AS A COLLEGE freshman, I attended journalism classes, had a spot on the student newspaper, studied French, and was a cheerleader for the football team. My journalism advisor said I had the makings of a fine reporter—as if he had picked up the script left by Ms. Nuxoll back in high school. He also said I should try to get an internship at the local newspaper. He promised to put in a good word for me.

ONE DAY IN the spring, I came home from classes, my pack over my shoulder and a bag of groceries in my arm. Patty waited on the steps with a letter in hand.

"I found her," Patty said. She had tears in her eyes.

Without knowing, I knew she meant her first mother. I dropped my things and we hugged in the narrow hall. Her door was wide open, as if she had been waiting for me. Mine remained locked.

"I can't believe how fast it happened," she said, over my shoulder. "I wrote to the agency, just like they told me to do, and a letter was waiting. My first mother wrote years ago."

She stepped back and wiped tears away with her fingertips. She looked proud, relieved, grateful, tired.

"My mother lives a few miles away, on a farm. She married my father, just after I was born but they couldn't get me back. They have been waiting my whole life. Can you believe it? I can't believe it. The whole thing feels surreal."

Her story was like a Disney fairytale. It was magical and amazing and even inspiring. I was happy for her, I was, but I didn't believe in Disney fairytales. My sensibility was more aligned with The Brothers Grimm.

I gathered up my groceries and my pack. "So, what now? Will you meet?"

"Yes," she said, "she wants to meet me, right away. Of course, I want to meet her too."

"Of course," I said. I unlocked my door. "That will be so great."

Inside, I turned on the lights in the living room, not the overhead, just the sconces and then the big brass lamp. In the dining room, I did the same thing—setting the lights on dim.

Patty followed me into my home, chattering about what had happened. I went to the kitchen, nodding and saying, "Uh huh." I turned on a lamp and put the groceries on the counter.

Finally, Patty stopped talking and let out a deep, satisfied sigh. She looked around the kitchen.

"Your place is always so clean. I don't know how you do it."

"It's just me," I said. "It's easy to keep clean."

"This is why I don't have you over. You would be appalled."

"No I wouldn't."

Patty leaned against the counter while I unloaded a carton of eggs, a stick of butter, and a half-gallon of milk. "You know," she said, "you should search too."

I laughed like that was a good one and stood in front of the open door of the refrigerator. "Do you want a beer?"

"Of course," she said.

I took out two beers, untwisted the tops, and passed one to her. Even though I was underage in Washington, I could buy beer and wine in Idaho, which was a thirty-minute drive. We clinked our bottles, said "Cheers" to her good news, and the beer sent a fast buzz into my arms and legs. I leaned against the edge of the counter like Patty.

"I mean it," Patty said. "I bet your mother is waiting for you too."

I wiped my mouth with the back of my hand and looked at my friend, drunk on her good fortune.

"What if she's not?" I asked.

"What if she is?" she countered.

"What if she's not?" I asked again. The sound of my voice was harder than I meant it to be.

Patty looked at me and I looked at her and she looked away first—unable to answer.

The end of our friendship was near.

EVEN THOUGH I thought I had forgotten Richard—he was soon in my life again in the form of a smart aleck guy named Jeff Means. Means. Can you imagine?

Jeff played football on the junior college team and would stare while I yelled out cheers from the sidelines.

"You've got the best legs I've ever seen," he'd say after every football game.

"You need glasses, buddy," I tell him.

He was a Class-A jerk.

WHEN WE STARTED dating, Jeff Means told me he wanted to play football but he knew it wasn't going to happen because he was too short.

Jeff was cute enough but he was so young, so boring, and he was doomed between the sheets. The guy didn't know up from down and was all over me like an overexcited puppy. I didn't have the heart to tell him how bad he was and instead endured whatever he was trying to do.

From the very beginning, I looked for a way to end it but Jeff was an amalgam of persistence and confidence. Jeff also insisted he loved me and that I would never find a guy like him again. I remember Richard saying a version of this to Peggy. *No one will love you like I do, Baby, heh heh heh.*

A part of me—the old, wise, and cynical part—knew that Jeff didn't love me. Jeff loved having sex with me. He also loved that I used birth control.

Another part of me, the part that kept going out with him and who was so hungry to be loved, wondered if he was right about never being loved again. I hadn't been loved up to this point—I had only been used. How would I know the difference?

In the beginning, I put up a good fight against Jeff and his intention to take complete occupation of my body, my home, and my life. I manufactured a story about being Catholic. I made a big deal about this spiritual affiliation, and with as much authority and mystery as I could conjure, I said being Catholic meant we couldn't live together. I explained that cohabitation was a *huge* sin. I added that people who lived together had to be married—not because I wanted to be married, I didn't. I said this to scare him.

When I moved from Richard and Peggy's, I packed my *Columbia Viking Desk Encyclopedia* set in a big box marked "childhood."

A few weeks after Patty found her mother—I unpacked the set. Under the letter C, I found the sheet that described my birth parents.

Mother: 17, blond hair, blue eyes, 5' 8.5", 128 pounds, English, Scottish, German, and Irish ancestry.

Father: 17, brunette, brown eyes, olive complexion, 5' 11", 160 pounds, German and Irish ancestry.

I don't know why I did it. It was insanity. A kind of self-mutilation. Emotional suicide.

I suppose what drove me was the *possibility* that my first mother might be out there waiting for me. Within Patty's success, I felt my cynicism—that great protector—finally slide aside. Like the tiny beating wings of a moth racing to the deadly light, I called the number on the top of the page and spoke to a woman in Nevada who worked at the Department of Child and Family Services. In a matter of moments, I was transferred to the adoption registry and a nice woman told me to write a letter. She said that if my first mother wrote a letter too, we'd be matched.

I wrote the letter.

A MONTH AFTER I sent the letter, I sat on my bed with the telephone on my lap. I called the Nevada Adoption Registry.

"Hello," a woman answered.

"Yes," I said, "I wrote a letter, um, let's see, about a month ago. I was just wondering if you received it and have a file in my name."

The lady put me on hold. I looked around my bedroom—just to have something to do. My bed was queen sized and covered with a soft comforter. There were pillows, from big to small—at least six—and at the end I kept a fuzzy throw. My favorite thing was to be in bed, reading and doing homework. I loved my bed.

The woman came back on the line and said yes, they had opened a file in my name.

I cleared my throat and forced words.

"Opened?" I asked. "Meaning you didn't have a file already? No one else has written?"

"Yes, that is correct. You are a new case."

"Case?"

"Adoptee making a request," she explained.

There was a thickness closing my throat, that predicable precursor to tears.

"No one has written?" I asked.

I knew the woman was probably rolling her eyes about the wack job on the line. How many times a day did she get this kind of call? Her voice was brisk and professional, as if we were talking about a deposit I made at my bank or a magazine subscription I submitted.

"No, not yet," she said.

"Are you sure?" I asked.

"Yes, ma'am," she said. "I'm sure."

I should've hung up. That was the most obvious next step but I didn't. I held the phone against my ear as if something else would happen. The lady said, "If you move, be sure to send in a change of address."

"Okay," I said.

"You know, having sex without being married is a sin too," Jeff said.

He was at my place, in my lovely bed, and we just had another round of his sloppy puppy sex. He was so happy and so oblivious. He had his hands behind his head.

I was at the edge of the bed, willing him to leave.

"My buddy at the store is Catholic and he says using birth control is a much bigger sin than living together."

I flushed with embarrassment and shame. He was talking about me at the RadioShack store? I considered this to be the perfect time to dump his ass. The words were at the tip of my tongue.

Jeff looked up at the ceiling, laughing a little—*heh heh heh*.

"Look, I don't care if we get married," he said. "I think we should. I'm just saying that before we get married, we should live together. It would save rent and I could work toward getting my own store. Being a manager at RadioShack is a great deal. You can make a ton of dough. My brother, you know, he's a regional manager and he says he'll help me get a step up."

Jeff closed the distance between us. He was muscled from lifting weights and exercising all the time. He was covered with little freckles and his hair, cut in the shape of a bowl, fell in his face.

"I was thinking about getting a store in Montana. That's big money. I want you with me. We could, you know, make a life."

"Is this supposed to be some kind of marriage proposal?"

"It could be," he said, "if you play your cards right."

I moved away from him. Another inch and I would have tumbled from my own bed.

"First, I have a life. I live here. I'm in school. I'm going to get an internship at the paper next year and I'm going to Eastern Washington University. Why would I change my plans and go to Montana?"

Jeff pushed his lower lip into a pout. He looked like he was ten years old. "For me," he said. "You know you couldn't live without me, Baby."

EVERY DAY, WHEN I came home, I checked my mail in hopes that a letter might come from Nevada. Every day I found an empty mailbox. Every day, I died a little death.

My mother was dead or she didn't have the courage to search or she didn't want to know how I was doing. All options—as I considered them in front of the empty mailbox—were devastating.

After three months of waiting, I made another call to the state of Nevada and spoke to the same lady at the adoption registry. I asked her to double-check that she had the correct birth date, place of birth, and delivering doctor. She said yes, they had all the information. She explained that if someone from my birth family sent an inquiry, she would let me know. "Try to be patient," she said.

Patient?

Twenty years isn't patient?

JEFF TOOK ME to dinner at a restaurant with linen tablecloths and candles. We sat at a table with a view of the waterfront and sunlight fell on the surface of the river, turning it into a mirror of the sky.

Jeff slid a velvet box between us. Even before I opened it, he said, "Please be my wife. Please marry me. I'll never love anyone more than I love you."

He wore a wool jacket from Sears. I helped him pick it out. It had leather patches on the elbows. He had been promoted to manager at RadioShack. He was twenty years old.

The ring in the box was a humble little solitaire in a silver and gold setting. Patty's engagement ring had been a glorious diamond that winked from a block away. It wasn't like I wanted a huge, flashy diamond. The difference though, in the rings, stood as a symbol of the difference between Patty and me. She knew she wanted to be married. She had a ring that made her jump up and down. I didn't want to be married and I had this tiny little diamond that screamed ambivalence.

Had I known anything about myself, I would have known that my mother married my father when she was nineteen. If I had been given some sense of her path, I would have seen that I was doing exactly what she had done and perhaps would have chosen differently for myself. But I knew nothing about my mother and her choices and thus knew nothing about myself. I was without a compass— although this is not completely true. My first compass, my first sense of being in this world, had been as an abandoned child whose mother did not hold her and later, did not search for her. Unloved. Yes, I had a strong sense that I was unloved and unlovable.

Who is closer to us than a mother but the lover? How hungry is the child who has not bonded with her mother? By nineteen, I was starving for human contact and for love. I didn't care if the human contact was cruel or painful or confused. That is why I endured Jeff and his fumbling attempt at closeness. That is why total occupation was inevitable.

"Okay," I finally said.

Jeff laughed, as if surprised, and I thought he was going to cry.

While he got himself together, clearing his throat and looking around to order dinner, I took the ring out of the box and slipped it on my own finger.

JUST BEFORE I married Jeff, I called the state of Nevada one last time. The lady at the registry lost patience with my questions. "Look," she snapped, "if someone writes a letter, we will call you."

SIX MONTHS AFTER the wedding, I graduated from the community college and was taking classes at Eastern Washington University.

Jeff had a store in the Spokane Valley and worked ninety hours a week. He still had ambitions to be transferred to a store in Montana. He said the profit margins were higher in remote locations and, now that we were married, he wanted to be closer to his mom and dad. Jeff also revealed that he wanted to start a family in Montana. He now wanted four boys—like his own mother had had.

Just as he had worn me down to the idea of sharing a home and being married, he was now trying to foist motherhood on my back. He was pressing me, unwittingly, to the edge of what would be possible. I wouldn't have one child with Jeff—let alone four. I wasn't becoming a mother and I certainly wasn't going to become a mother with Jeff. My best friend was the birth control pill—which I took like religion—every single day.

I WAS HOME when the long-distance call came from Nevada. As the line crackled with that familiar sound of the far away, I thought: *This is it. My mother.*

But the voice belonged to a cousin named Tracy who lived in Carson City. She was one of Auntie Carol's kids.

"I haven't talked to you for years," I said. "How are you doing?"

Tracy's voice was high and full of emotion. She got right to the point. Bryan had disappeared three days earlier. The Lauck family had been frantic trying to figure out where he went and she wanted to know if I had seen him.

"Me? No. Why?"

"I don't know," she said, "just a wild guess. We've called everyone else and I thought maybe you'd know."

"You've called everyone else before me? You mean the whole family knows Bryan is missing? How long? How long have you known?"

"A couple days, I guess. Look, it's not personal."

I sat down at the dining table and the cord of the phone pulled tight.

Bryan had been at my wedding. He came from Oklahoma and we had a couple of conversations, brief and jagged. He said he had been at a seminary in Missouri, studying to be a priest but that didn't work out. He planned to go to the University of Oklahoma to finish a degree in philosophy. I asked what he'd do with a degree in philosophy. He laughed for a long time. He said I made a good point.

I had no point. I just wanted to know.

BRYAN AND I were strangers. With all the years of being separated, we had no common ground except the losses in our past and to Bryan's mind, they weren't my losses. They were his. And he was suffering. He said he felt depressed and sad. "You're lucky you were adopted," he said. "In a way, you are exempt."

When Bryan and I parted, a dark thought entered my mind. *That's the kind of guy who could end up killing himself.* I even said this to Jeff, as we left for our honeymoon. Jeff just shrugged as if he didn't know and didn't care. He didn't know Bryan. He wasn't interested in more than his plan to get to Montana and to begin that big family of boys.

WHILE TRACY AND I talked, the dark thought of suicide returned and grew into a knowing. I knew. Bryan was dead. My brother had killed himself.

THERE WERE TWO tracks of experience. On one, I searched for my first mother. On another, my brother did, in fact, kill himself.

On the first track, my mother was not looking for me. Even though the Nevada registry had been open for reunions for many years, she hadn't written a letter. My father hadn't either.

On the second track, Bryan was dead. He had been the last living relative from my immediate family, the last link to the chain.

I FLEW TO an impoverished and remote town in Oklahoma—where Bryan grew up with Uncle Larry and Aunt Ruth—and attended the funeral. Jeff didn't come. "Why?" he had asked. "I didn't know the guy."

The soil of Oklahoma was red clay and the air was humid and thick enough to scoop in my hands. Uncle Larry (Bud's younger brother) and his wife Ruth were both wrapped tight in a resigned state of poverty. Larry had been released from his military commission during cutbacks. The government had betrayed them. I saw, with vivid clarity, that Bryan did not have a happy life.

AT THE FUNERAL, Uncle Larry introduced me as Bryan's adopted sister. I was placed in a pew a few rows back from the Lauck family. Aunt Peggy had, no doubt, told Larry that I had been insubordinate and needed to be distanced from the Lauck clan.

I held my hands in my lap and stared holes into my brother's casket. It was a wood box that had been sealed. Bryan had apparently been outside for many days after he shot himself. His body was not fit to view.

In my head, madness played a little film where I stomped to the front of the church, threw open the casket, and yelled, "My brother is not dead."

The desire to jump up and set the record straight was overpowering. I had to hug myself to stay put. I talked myself down. I told myself to knock it off and lay low.

IN FACT, I did have a living brother. My brother, the son of my birth mother and birth father, lived in Reno and was growing up healthy and happy. He was just two years younger than me.

The moment of madness that had overtaken me in the church that day stayed with me like an unsolved puzzle for years. I had a knowing at a cellular level, and this knowing created distinct tension and anxiety. I felt the way you feel when you are being lied to but the liar won't admit it. It was a dissonant knowing.

For years—hauling this memory of Bryan's funeral around—I thought I had been a madwoman going through some extraordinary grieving process. When I returned from the funeral, I went to bed. I didn't eat. I dropped out of school. I didn't speak. All I could do was weep until I passed out. When I woke up, I started the cycle over again.

Infants are unable to regulate their own emotions; they need their mother's response to their cries to teach them mood normalization. And the infant doesn't wait for any mother, she waits for her birth mother—the one with which she shared a hormonal connection while in utero. Any other caregiver is rejected.

It's a terrible plight. A baby must endure biological and mental torture. She experiences terror, goes into shock (due to the abandonment), and loses consciousness—again and again.

Since the brain is built on experience, synapses making permanent connections, these first feelings are foundational patterns that are nearly impossible to eradicate. The brain seeks out what it knows and deepens the patterns with repetition.

After Bryan's funeral, I was repeating that first trauma. This is how I know I was not grieving for Bryan. I was grieving for my birth mother, all over again.

If we are talking about cause and effect—karma—what is the energetic power of the traumatized brain? Is it a force of its own, like a magnet that drags terrorizing circumstances, people, and events into its path in order to reexperience traumatic responses that have become familiar and even comforting? If terror is what the mind knows, is terror then sought out? Is this how predators identify victims? Is this power what attracts cruel people into the lives of trauma victims and has them stick around year after brutal year? Had my brain—with its unique wiring and built-in responses—been drawing me into situations that resulted in rape, abuse, neglect, and cruelty?

JEFF WAS PROMOTED to a store in Montana and before he left, he came to the bed where I continued my decline and told me to snap out of it.

"Enough already," he said. "You didn't even like your brother."

He was right, I didn't like Bryan—the guy had been cruel to me but I told myself that Bryan was all I had left of my first family and now he was gone. I told myself I was just grieving.

I couldn't possibly factor in deep, prememory feelings that pointed toward that infant trauma. No one spoke of adoptees and their silent sorrows. We were acquired, assimilated, and adapted. Our histories were hidden from us and our memories were a muddled mess—like our lives—like my own life. All I knew at the age of twenty was that I was in pain and no one could help me. I considered suicide as an escape.

WHAT PULLED ME out of the terrible loop was a small dog—a puppy.

I had gone to a U-Haul store to get boxes and heard the sound of barking coming from a nearby store.

Spokane Pet Center had a new batch of cocker spaniel pups and there she was: a tiny runt who cowered in the corner of pine chips. I scooped the pup in my hand—this little warm ball of fluff—and the name Carmel popped into my head.

"Come home with me," I said to the little creature with the huge brown eyes and the gentle manner. "Let me take care of you."

SIXTEEN

THREE YEARS LATER

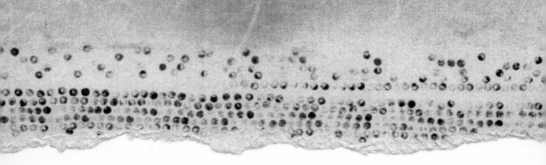

I MOVED BACK to Spokane, Washington, and my roommate was a full-grown Carmel.

Jeff stayed at his RadioShack store, adding up the profits and making new plans. Not more than a year after I left, he was married and on his way to making those four boys.

What ended it?

I did.

He was mean. He punched Carmel in a fit of rage and I was pretty sure I would have been next.

There were three gifts in knowing Jeff. One was that I didn't conceive a child with him.

Two was that, thanks to a divorce procedure that allowed a name change, I became Jennifer Caste Lauck again.

Three, I used my short time in Montana to become an investigative reporter.

As soon as I arrived in Billings, at the far eastern edge of that

Big Sky State, I mothered Carmel to full doghood and also worked toward my degree in journalism at Eastern Montana College. In less than two years, I had elbowed my way into an internship at a TV station and then became a reporter for the Montana Television Network.

While Jeff worked at his RadioShack store in the Rim Rock Mall, I was the one who reported about grasshopper infestations and bank robberies on the evening news. You would have seen me at the snowy sight of a plane crash—a mail plane—where the pilot died. Fires, abductions, marijuana busts—yes, I was there. I was the one with the microphone and the snazzy short hair cut.

Jeff wanted his woman to stay home and make babies. My success infuriated him.

After the marriage vaporized, I accepted a promotion at a television station in Spokane. I couldn't leave him or Montana fast enough.

As a single woman, my ambitions became like a detonation within my imagination. I planned to stay in Spokane for a year or so, get a promotion to a station in Seattle or maybe Portland, Oregon, and then I'd be off to Los Angeles or perhaps New York. I could see myself working for the network or maybe becoming a foreign correspondent. I envisioned bullets whizzing overhead as I reported, live, from some trench in the desert. I'd be the first one to tell you how it was on the battle lines. I'd bring you the news you needed to know. I'd tell you the truth.

But then I met Steve.

SEVENTEEN

THE BIG FIGHT

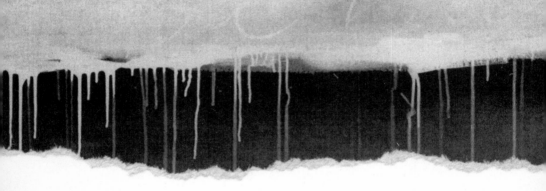

THERE ARE SOME STORIES you can tell and others that you have no business telling, and that's how it is with Steve.

In the end, he's the father of Spencer and Jo and that's the best part of the story. He walked with me into parenthood. He convinced me I could be a better mother than how I had been mothered. Steve had faith in me when I didn't have faith in myself. That was the gift. The worst part of the story is that Steve and I couldn't make it. We divorced when Spencer was seven and Jo was two.

The part I don't know if I can tell is *why* we ended. I want to say it was the fighting. Steve and I argued all the time, over stupid things like paint chips, what movie to watch, and where to eat dinner. But I don't know.

What are the details that add up to divorce? How can we map such a complex topography as that of the interior of two souls who make vows, intermingle, and create life from one another? In the end, isn't marriage this puzzlement of staring at each other over cups of coffee while wondering, *Who the hell are you?* Isn't it true that to be married to another is to know you look at a stranger everyday? Can't we all say that no matter how much we *think* we know another person, we don't; we can't? Isn't a human being simply too vast and too deep to define and to know?

Or perhaps I've got it all wrong. Perhaps the truth of Steve and me and our end lies within me. After all, did I have any idea who I was? In living with myself, didn't I look at a stranger in the mirror everyday? Wasn't it true that no matter how much I *thought* I knew who I was, I didn't; I couldn't?

WHEN I MET Steve, it was 1987. He was twenty-seven years old and I was twenty-four.

Steve was a tall, good-looking guy with dark hair and medium-blue eyes that gave off a metallic spark when he smiled. He had a good sense of humor and could always make me laugh. Steve was also a part-time student, just finishing his degree, and for money, he worked for a company that auctioned collectable cars.

His last name was Dorsey and I always called him the Dors-man.

The Dors-man grew up in the Spokane Valley and lived in the same house nearly all his life. His parents were quiet people who kept to themselves, and nothing, other than the weather and the seasons and time, changed in their lives. Steve's mom was a cake decorator. Steve's dad repaired tractor engines. He had a younger sister. Steve was the oldest.

In our early days together, I worked as reporter for an ABC

station in town and covered hard news—murders, drug busts, fires. It was good work—exciting and a little dangerous too—but at the end of the day, telling stories that had no happy ending made me tired. Human suffering wore me down.

Eventually, I took a job in Portland, Oregon, at another ABC station and Steve found a job with an auction company nearby.

Six years into each other, we got married. We would both agree this was an odd decision, considering our proclivity toward tension, which had us bickering most of the time.

We had this attraction—a live wire of energy ran between us—and arguing amped up the charge. I suppose we were addicted to each other or to the tension of our connection.

Once married, with the idea that perhaps we would start a family, I stopped working in TV and Steve and I bought an old house on a street that straddled the line between two neighborhoods called Rose City and Hollywood.

IT WAS A Sunday afternoon in 1994 and we had spent ten hours painting the living room a shade that tried to be linen yellow but looked—to me—more like lemon. Steve was in coveralls and splattered with the disappointing paint that made me think of preschool.

I wore jeans and an old work shirt.

I took a stand against the color.

Steve insisted it was fine.

I wanted to change it.

He wanted to leave it.

I pushed.

He shoved.

After three rounds, I dropped my end of the argument and dissolved into tears.

"I can't believe we are arguing over paint," I yelled through my tears. "I don't even know what I'm doing here. I never wanted to move into this ramshackle house to begin with."

Steve threw his hands up over his head and paced the room while he yelled at the walls.

"Oh, great, here we go again. Now you don't want to live here, now you didn't want to move. Now it's all my fault since it was my idea to buy the damn house."

My old dog, Carmel, was on the bed between us, hunched low with her snout on her paws. Her slow brown eyes shifted from Steve to me.

"Oh Steve, shut up."

Carmel shifted her gaze over to Steve.

"Shut up! Are you telling me to shut up?"

"Yes, Jesus! Shut up! I'm crying here! What kind of man yells at his wife while she is crying?"

"I get it, I get it now. You don't think I'm a good enough man. Now it's just not about the house, it's about being my wife. Just admit it, Jennifer. You didn't want to move into this house and you didn't want to get married."

"Would you just shut up, Steve? Stop yelling at me. I can't think."

Carmel jumped off the bed and nosed her way into the closet. In the dark and quiet place, she settled in and listened to us scream.

IN THERAPY, THEY say that couples usually have one core issue they argue about. This was our fight. I was ambivalent about my life choices, which included being married and moving into an old house that needed years of hard work. I was ambivalent about most things. Absolute certainty belonged to others but I had not discovered that quality within myself. Steve, whose middle name might as well have been "confident," just happened to be in the mix of my story of uncertainty.

Steve took my ambivalence personally. He would blame himself, as if he were responsible for my happiness.

A therapy session between us might go like this:

Therapist: What Jennifer is saying, Steve, is that she feels uncertain and even lost a great deal of the time. How does that make you feel?

Steve: Well, that's bullshit. Look at her, she's confident. She knows what she wants. She makes decisions. Jennifer is tough and strong. She's a real go-getter.

Therapist: Are you sure that is who Jennifer is? Are you seeing the real Jennifer or your image of Jennifer?

Steve: (Tosses a dirty look at Jennifer since he didn't want to do therapy in the first place. He shifts in his chair. He crosses one leg over the other.)

Therapist: (Observes tension between couple and defensive posture of Steve.) Let's try a different approach. Steve, why don't you describe your wife.

Steve: I don't get it.

Therapist: As if she isn't here. Just tell me who you think Jennifer is.

Steve: Well, that's easy. First, she is a woman, obviously. She's tall, great legs, good cook, confident, hardworking. She's my wife. We have two kids. She's smart. Really smart.

Jennifer: (Laughs.)

Steve: What? It's true. You're smart. Hell, you're smarter than me.

Jennifer: Don't put yourself down. You're always putting yourself down.

Steve: I don't always put myself down.

Jennifer: You do too. He does.

Therapist: (Hands up.) Okay, hold on. Let's stay on Steve and the question.

Steve: (Frowns, shakes his head. Doesn't remember question.)

Therapist: What else do you see when you look at Jennifer?

Jennifer: (Restless with therapist. Thinks he is a hack.) The dark stuff, Steve. He wants to know the deeper things. What pisses you off about me?

Steve: (Nods, grateful for the translation.)

Therapist: (Gives Jennifer a small nod too. Makes a note on his pad, *Jennifer = controlling*.)

Steve: (Shifts in his chair, looks at ground. Passes glance over to Jennifer.) Are you sure you want to hear it, Jen? Do you really want to go there?

Jennifer: You're not telling me, you're telling him. Tell him. Who am I?

Therapist: (Looks at Jennifer for a long moment. Considers asking her to leave room.)

Steve: (Takes a deep breath and rubs his face.) Well, I guess I would say Jennifer is one of those people, you know, she's sad.

Therapist: (Perks up again, makes notes.) Can you tell me more? Can you tell me more about this sadness you see?

Steve: (Looks at Jennifer with more concern.)

Jennifer: (Nods as if Steve should continue.)

Steve: (Clears his throat and coughs into his fist.) Well, when Jennifer gets sad, it's hard. It's like she turns around and disappears— even though she's right in front of me.

Therapist: (Leans forward in chair.) How does that make you feel?

Steve: (Looks at therapist—hard—looks at Jennifer, looks at his own shoes, looks at time on watch. Thinks about how this session is costing him two hundred and fifty bucks.) Well, I guess I want to pull her out of wherever she goes, out of her sadness—I want to be like the guy who saves the day—you know, the hero who rides in on a horse. I guess I just want to be the one who makes Jennifer happy.

Therapist: (Takes furious notes, both congratulating himself on a job well done and also getting ready to ask Steve about his childhood and his relationship to his own mother.)

Jennifer: (Crying.)

Steve: (Furious with himself. Thinking, *Great, now I've made her cry.*)

AFTER ELEVEN YEARS together and a good amount of therapy, Steve didn't really want to look at his need to rescue me and to take it so personally. He didn't want to talk about his mother and his past either. For Steve, childhood belonged back in childhood. He was from Spokane, for heaven's sake. No one did therapy in Spokane.

Steve and I went on with our lives, we argued about paint chips, movies, and where to eat dinner. I continued to feel lost and ambivalent, and I continued to go away, deep into myself—after all I was writing a memoir. And Steve continued to believe that I was going away from him, that I didn't want to be with him or our children. He felt he had failed me.

In the end, when I left our marriage, I told him I just had to keep looking for that missing something.

"Looking for what?" Steve would always ask. "What are you looking for, Jen?"

EIGHTEEN

THE JOURNEY

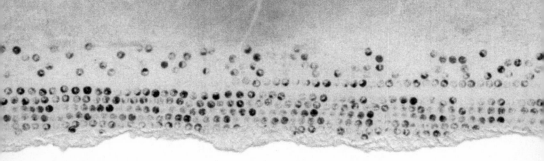

WHEN HE WAS in town, Steve stayed in the house overnight and I slept at my office, a few blocks away. When he was out of town, I'd sleep in the basement.

This was not an arrangement he created. I was the one to put myself on the outside and to put Steve on the inside with our kids. I cast myself out as the failure.

On the nights I was away from my home, the routine, and the children, I was so unhappy, I'd curl up into a fetal position and cry for the physical pain I felt in missing my own children.

"Come home, Jen," Steve would say, but I had to batter myself. My mind fed me lines of failure that buried me deeper and deeper still. "You're trash. You blew it. It's all your fault."

I cried until I passed out.

BEFORE, IT HAD been Carmel who saved my life. But since Carmel had died of old age—a few years earlier—the task of calling me out of my habitual loop of self-torment fell to Spencer.

While I walked him to school, pretending all was well, Spencer tugged on my hand. "Mom," he said, "I can't find you."

We were on the way to his second-grade classroom. His teacher, Beth, stood at the door and shook hands with another child. We were next.

I did a quick U-turn and maneuvered into a stairwell. I collapsed on the sticky, dirty stairs and held his upper arms. I looked into his dark chocolate eyes. "What do you mean, Sweets?" I asked.

"I look for you, at night. I go through the house and you're not anywhere."

Spencer, seven years old, had dark, shining hair cut in the shape of a bowl and a long, angular face.

"What about Jo?" I asked. "Is she awake at night too?"

"I don't think so," he said. "You know Jo. She's always so happy."

The school bell rang but we didn't move off the steps.

I chewed the edge of my lip. How to fit this huge news into a small headline? "Well, Sweetie, Dad and I aren't getting along so great and I've been sleeping at my office," I finally admitted. "I'm sorry. I should have told you."

I smoothed his hair and Spencer looked relieved. A part of him knew.

"I want to sleep where you sleep," he said. "Can I come to your office too?"

His longing, so pure and raw, made me so sad. Hadn't I learned that children know everything, feel everything?

I hugged him close and promised that yes, he could, but I would also go to work and find a place of my own. "I'll find a house," I said. "I'll make a place for us to be together."

"When?" he asked.

"Right now," I said. "Today."

"Good," he said.

I FOUND A house just a few blocks from Steve, made a down payment, and created a new home. I bought all new things so moving was like a party for the kids—a time of expansion—and not a funeral march through divorce.

I circled tight around their routine and recreated myself around their needs.

Jo was just two and a half. Spencer neared eight.

Jo had her art projects and Mommy and Me classes. Spence had school and play dates. We had dinnertime and reading time and bedtime. Mundane activities like brushing teeth, taking baths, and folding clothes were my sanity. I buried myself in their schedule as if in a cave—belowground.

Lovers entered and exited. These men started as momentary comfort and became monotonous and suffocating. I seemed to attract a long line of losers who were needy, clingy, and even abusive. I found a poignant passage by Nor Hall, who wrote *The Moon and the Virgin*, and with a Sharpie pen I transcribed the words on the wall over my bed:

> *The virgin forest is not barren or unfertilized but rather a place*
> *that is especially fruitful and has multiplied because it has*

taken life into itself and transformed it, giving birth naturally and taking dead things back to be recycled. It is virgin because it is unexploited, not in man's control.

The passage stood as a warning to all lovers: You are temporary! Do not settle in.

My internal state became that of a virgin.

This began what some might call the spiritual journey. That is, the call to the spirit within—or perhaps the soul of a person—or the soul of everything. I now entered the deepest part of the quest toward the elusive and the unknown.

This is when I discovered meditation and a teacher of meditation named Tylanni Drolma.

TYLANNI DROLMA. TYLANNI. While I didn't know what her name meant, the sound of it contained worlds unknown. At first I found a series of meditation tapes she had recorded called *Awaken from Fear.* I listened to these tapes—over and over again—not just for the meditation she offered but also for the story she told of her life. Tylanni had traveled through India and Tibet, had been a nun in the Tibetan tradition of Buddhism and then went on to marry—not once, but twice—and had several children.

I thought, *Here's a woman who has traveled deep into the complexities of marriage and motherhood and even into spirituality.* I needed such a guide at this stage of my own life.

I ordered her book titled *Illusion's Wake Up Call* and when it arrived, paged directly to the center to find a photo of Tylanni Drolma as a young woman. Her hair had been shaved—traditional for someone who had taken the vows of a nun. She held a bundle of wool blankets. As I stared into this grainy image, my body was covered with chills. I told myself I had to speak to her.

I learned, via Internet research, that Tylanni lived in Canada. She ran a retreat center called The Pure Land.

The name itself felt mysterious and vast—like the sea. I was speechless and also felt called to action.

I wrote a quick email: "I read your book. I wanted to ask how you were able to maintain a spiritual life and be a mother."

Within hours, Tylanni typed a return email. "Come to Canada, perhaps take the Tara retreat, and we shall talk about this."

Her message was so surprising and yet also felt so important—although I had no inkling why. All I could do—as if something larger than myself was driving forward momentum—was to arrange childcare, book a ticket, and make the trip.

To THE AVERAGE city dweller, getting to The Pure Land is not easy. You have to take a plane to Calgary and a puddle jumper to Golden (and keep hold of the barf bag because it's a brutal, bumpy flight). Next, you make an hour trek to Jasper and another hour trip on unpaved roads. Make a hard right and cut through raw forestland on a one-way double-track trail. Be careful of the huge boulders, don't careen your rig into the creek, and keep your eyes on the horizon—in search of silk prayer flags.

When you get to The Pure Land (if you get there), know that you are someone who wanted to get there. It takes serious focus to make that journey, and it takes serious commitment to stay.

When I arrived that first time, I thought to myself, *what the hell am I doing here?*

My only religious training—which I had walked away from—was in the Catholic Church. In my twenties, with my mean first husband, I had dipped into the vat of ecstatic Christianity and accepted Jesus Christ, our Lord and Savior, into my heart. I just loved that phrase—*Jesuschristourlordandsavior.* When I said it, over and over again, it felt like being born. Eventually I made my way back to the more subdued and stern Catholics where there were absolutes like: *If you do bad things you burn in hell* and *God is up there and we are down here.* I had my first marriage annulled by a Catholic council, just to play by the rules, and even though I didn't go to church (the whole perspective on women bummed me out), I did consider myself to be a faithful person. I believed in forces bigger than myself. I believed in divine intervention. I could count off several moments in my own life where I felt the power of Grace. But my faith was my business. Religion felt very personal.

I suppose I could say that I arrived at The Pure Land with an open heart. I was ready to believe I had come for a divine reason that would be revealed. But it also fair to say, on the issue of religion, I was skeptical too.

THE PURE LAND had rolling hills, open meadows, a few yurts, and a lean-to style kitchen built among the leaning trunks of aspen and pines. Upon arrival, I was assigned to a dusty tent, ate a bit of wilted salad, and found my way to the first teaching.

In hiking boots, I clomped up a gravel road that ended at the double doors of a canvas yurt.

Inside, the air was thick with incense and candles burned around a circular altar where a dozen statues of the same beautiful jade green woman were arranged in a circle. On the lattice walls, there were silk paintings of Asian men and women dancing, sitting cross-legged, and even making love. All I had ever seen were statues of a pious Mary, head bowed in contemplative sorrow, and Christ ratcheted to a cross, his face distorted in eternal pain. I found myself staring at the Tibetan interpretation of the Divinity with a voyeur's curiosity.

At the back of the yurt, *the* Tylanni Drolma sat on a pile of cushions and sheep skins. I stopped looking around and stared at her.

The Tylanni Drolma was a small, dark-haired woman wrapped in a prayer shawl. She had a serene smile and vivid amber eyes.

While I had never been one to place another on a pedestal—I didn't have a penchant for celebrity—Tylanni had been elevated to star status in my own psyche.

I found my way to the back of the yurt and eased to a cushion on the floor, all the while staring at this woman, this VIP.

With all the buildup in my mind, I had expected rockets to explode upon seeing her, but nothing happened. She didn't even look my way. I was just one of a dozen people—a stranger.

As the retreat progressed, Tylanni taught the history of Tara. She was the Buddha of compassionate action, born from the tear of another Buddha. In one story, Tara was a princess who reached enlightenment at a time when it was believed women couldn't be enlightened. Tylanni told us that meditation on Tara could bring good fortune and remove obstacles.

I realized early on that it wasn't Tylanni who drew me. It was Tara, and as soon as I learned some basic history, I was a goner. I filled pages of my journal from Tylanni's lectures. I thought it was just great that this woman—this Tara—existed in the annals of women's history. I liked to think it was possible, even provable, that women were capable of active divinity and not just passive acceptance. Whereas the Virgin Mary, in my own mind, kept everything in her heart, Tara was a woman who got the job done. Tara was a powerhouse of compassion with a purpose. Tara was the Go-To Girl. Yes, I liked Tara right away.

After the history of Tara, Tylanni taught the Green Tara meditation practice, which included a series of prayers and visualizations where you imagined yourself as Tara. It was like a kid playing dress-up. Visualization was just an invitation to use your imagination. Giving up my identity as Jennifer, mother, soon to be ex-wife, sad girl, and orphan was a welcome fantasy.

Tylanni led the practice, and like learning dance steps, it was awkward at first. I worried that I stuck out like a sore thumb but everyone was new to Tara. We were all learning the moves.

Once we arrived at the section of the meditation where we repeated the mantra—a kind of prayer—in our minds, I became quite calm for a long while.

Mantra is a short phrase you say again and again, and this mantra was *Om Tare Tut Tare*. It had a complex meaning I was trying to remember when I felt such an odd thing. As I silently said *Om Tare* to myself, I felt as if I were being pulled apart. A desperate feeling rose within me—I had this need to reclaim my former identity. I wanted to call out, "I am Jennifer Lauck. I am a writer." I wanted to stand up and declare this identity to the room. It was so odd, and then, like plastic wrap being pulled from a Jell-O mold, the identity of being a writer just slipped away.

Om Tare continued to circle my mind and I thought, *I am Tara*. It was not like being Tara as Tylanni described. I was not a teardrop of compassion or a princess. I certainly wasn't some green jade woman. But there was, for the first time, certainty. I was certain that I was Tara. I knew it was true. I was.

This revelation was both wonderful and terrible.

I opened my eyes and looked around at the yurt, the altar, the candles, and Tylanni, and I thought, *What the hell just happened?*

I closed my eyes again and the same certainty returned.

I was Tara.

As if it wasn't enough to become a jade green deity that dated back to 500 BC, I also felt emotion rise within my body. I felt sadness unlike any I had ever felt before.

Steve used to call me a sad woman but the word "sad" felt paltry when compared to the apocalypse of sorrow thundering up from the core of my own body.

Tossing the Tara booklet on the meditation table, I stood up and made my way out the door. On the front porch of the yurt—snow topped Canadian Rocky Mountains in the distance—I pulled on my hiking boots and made tracks into the hills. Down a deep ravine, up a hill, down into another ravine, and up one more hill.

When I could no longer run, I hit the ground and sobs wracked through my body with such stunning force, all I could do was let them have their way.

Lord, did I cry and the whole time, sobbing and rolling from the power of my own grief, all I could do was watch myself in wonder. I had been holding all that sadness in my body—my small 150-pound self—how was that possible?

If I had seen a woman cry like I was crying that day, I would have called 9-1-1. It was crushing to see such a display of a broken heart. I had no idea.

EVENTUALLY, WHEN THE tears were done and I was spent, I stumbled back to the yurt. With puffy eyes, I took my place in the back of the room and listened to the others who were now in the question-and-answer phase of the teaching.

After a bit of time passed and no one seemed to be covering the question of cosmic grief, I asked about the sadness I had felt and if such strong emotion was common in spiritual practice.

Tylanni regarded me for a long time. Her eyes were so golden and so steady. Finally, she said that meditation, especially on Tara, could bring "a lot" up in people.

Not to be brushed off, I asked another question. I wanted to know what specifically was coming up, not that "a lot" was coming up.

Tylanni smiled—indulgent perhaps—and suggested that I just relax and keep practicing.

NINETEEN

PRACTICE

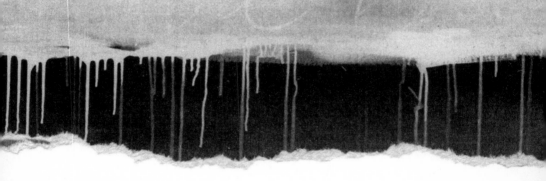

"YOU'RE GOING AGAIN?"

Steve was incredulous.

"Yes," I said. "It takes time."

"How hard is it to meditate?"

"Hard."

We stood at the back gate of my new house and he had just brought the kids home from school. They scurried under my arm and into the house with kisses, hugs, and cries of "What's for dinner?" and "See you later, Dad!"

"I leave next Saturday, Steve, it's just a few days."

I moved to close the gate, conversation over, but Steve stopped me.

"Is this about a guy? Are you going with a guy?"

"No," I said. "No guy. Just meditation. That's all."

"I just don't get it. You are a Catholic for god's sake."

"I'm not a Catholic," I said, defensive. "I was a Catholic."

"Whatever. I still don't get it."

"Why do you care?"

"Well, for the kids," he said. "I want to make sure it's not some cult, where you all go off and drink poison Kool-Aid or something."

We looked at each other and I knew he didn't think I was into a cult. He was just taking it personally. My new path was leading further away from him. He knew it; I knew it. What could I say?

"I'm going. I'll be back in a few days."

I pulled the gate closed. Steve didn't stop me.

I TRAVELED TO The Pure Land four times that summer of 2004. Each trip, usually about four days, taught me another Tibetan practice: Guru Yoga, Mandala of the Dakini, The Five Buddha Families. But it was Tara that I loved. I couldn't do Tara practice enough.

Tylanni—as the door to Tara—became beloved. If I came within three feet of her, I would cry like a fool.

Tylanni, moved by my intense emotion, was gentle and supportive—very much the caring mother. "I cried every time I thought about my first guru too," she said.

As part of my newfound devotion to Tara and to Tylanni, I took what was called Refuge. In Buddhism, like most religions, there are rules to follow: don't kill, don't lie, don't steal, don't get drunk, don't gossip. That kind of thing. When you take Refuge, you agree to follow the rules.

As part of taking Refuge, I was also given a Buddhist name

and I was sure it would be Tara and whatever word stood for "writer" in Tibetan. After all, I loved Tara and I was a writer. It made sense.

Tylanni named me Jampel Sherab, which meant expansive love of transcendent wisdom, or the innate quality of wisdom that cuts through to the truth. While it rang true, I was not looking for my future self, I was looking for some recognizable core self.

I took Tylanni's offered name, that Jampel Sherab, and shoved myself towards the lofty ambitions such a name seemed to hold. I even gave Tylanni the pearls that had once been passed to me by Auntie Carol as if to say Janet was no longer my mother. I told myself I was now a different kind of daughter who was learning at the feet of a different kind of mother, one who I believed expected me to be expansive and transcendent.

Looking back, I see I was—in large part—accepting a different version of the same divinity that my first mother, Janet, had foisted on my back. I was binding my fragile self to a living woman—Tylanni—who needed help to build the multimillion-dollar retreat center. As part of our relationship, I willingly cleaned toilets, scrubbed floors, made meals, and handed over huge amounts of time and money. I did everything I was asked and more. I couldn't do enough. I lived in dread of letting Tylanni down. I wasn't in a relationship of choice, I was in a relationship of need—for mother, for acceptance, for family, and for home.

It had been Janet and Bud who had set me up to fail as divine daughter. What child can save a dying woman?

Now, I was setting myself up for failure and it was coming faster than I knew.

OVER THE NEXT year, through fall, winter, and spring, I almost exclusively practiced meditation. I didn't write. I didn't date. I didn't even pursue friendships.

My children added inches to their height, pounds to their bodies, and words to their expanding vocabularies. Steve and I found the common ground of caring for their needs, and I was a mother and a yogini.

You could find me in the grocery store, shopping for our weekly supplies and you could find me in the mountains of Calgary where I'd take weekend retreats (while the kids were with Steve).

As my practice progressed, I'd sometimes take the kids along to The Pure Land and we'd camp together in tents tied to the aspens and pines.

Spencer became very fond of Tylanni and spent time hiking the trails around the land. Josephine was happy to be close to me, rearranging the altar while I meditated or off picking wildflowers, which she piled in my lap.

For three years, I lived split between Oregon and Canada, between the demands of being a spiritual student and the demands of motherhood, between my desire to become fully enlightened and the reality of my own flawed humanity.

I WOULD HAVE been happy doing Tara meditation—just Tara. I was a complete devotee. I had a Tara tattoo on my hip and my license plate read *Om Tara*. The kids knew that mantra by heart and we'd sing it together when we took baths or long rides in the car.

But a student of Tibetan Buddhism is expected—some might say pressed—into other practices. Nothing remains static.

Tylanni eventually encouraged me to study with a master from Tibet. His name was Rinpoche. Tylanni also suggested I get going on a basic practice that all students were required to do: Ngondro (noon-drow).

Think about plowing hard ground loaded with rocks. That's Ngondro.

Ngondro also means you are going to spend two solid years of your life—if you work damn hard—digging into your own human soil and turning it soft and fine so it can grow a sustainable crop.

NGONDRO, FIVE SEPARATE meditations combined into one, included prayers and mantras for purification (imagine cleaning out your house), for accumulating what is called merit (like putting money in a savings account), and for requesting divine help (picture Moses praying to God for strength before springing the Jews from Egypt).

To know if Ngondro was working—that is, if I was doing it right and getting the benefit of the meditation—I was alerted to look for rainbows and peacocks within my own dreams. To have these markers meant I was making real strides.

As I practiced Ngondro each day, through the next two years, the walls of my room at home became papered with drawings that

Jo turned out by the dozen each day. Each of them contained a rainbow and some had peacocks too. I didn't even notice. I was so split in my own attentions, I failed to make the connection between her art and my practice. I'd tape her pages into place, praising her with hugs and kisses, and carried on as if my meditation and Jo were separate.

IN THE SUMMER of 2007, Rinpoche came to Canada. Of course, I booked my ticket to see him. That was part of the drill. Meet the master, give a status update, receive blessings and instruction.

After three years of my devotions to Tara, Tylanni, and Buddhism, Steve had finally stopped asking questions. He booked his vacations with the kids to fall at the same time I needed to go into retreat. He said he didn't understand what I was doing but like me, he thought maybe, just maybe I had found what I was looking for.

AT THE PURE Land that summer, I set up my solo camp in the scrub oaks, and with more than one hundred of my fellow students, awaited the arrival of Rinpoche.

He was coming from Tibet, via China and then by way of Germany. He wasn't the Dalai Lama but in spiritual circles, our Rinpoche was like a rock star. It was said that he saw upwards to 400,000 students a year.

The night before his arrival, there were rainbow rings around the moon—an auspicious sign.

Under that moon, I couldn't sleep and hiked through sagebrush and shadows to the practice yurt. At that hour, 3:00 AM, the yurt was empty and cold. All the meditation cushions were stacked against one wall. Tiny mice raced across the floor in a scramble of wild claws and disappeared under the floorboards.

I lit a few candles—enough to get the place glowing—and went to work on the physical part of the Ngondro called prostrations. You dive to the ground, press your body flat and touch your forehead to the floor. Next you push back and stand up again. You do this—count them—one hundred and eight thousand times. 108,000.

Over the first three months, I had accumulated more than twenty thousand prostrations. I could usually do about two hundred and fifty a day, but in the yurt that night I did three hundred and couldn't stop.

The sunrise stained the white snow peaks of the Rockies with the colors of silver and pink and I entered an endorphin high runners call "the zone." My body was slick with sweat and my breath hit an even pace. Five hundred.

As the sun exploded into the wide blue sky, the only sound was the thump of my body as it slapped down and slid over the smooth wooden floor. Every six seconds, I was down and up again and then down once more. Seven hundred and fifty.

My imagination held the visualization of all my families—known and unknown. I conjured Steve, the children, Richard, Peggy, Deb and her children, Bryan, Janet, and Bud. I even imagined my first mother and first father—whoever and wherever they were. I thought of all the faceless connected to me: siblings, aunts, uncles, grandparents, great grandparents. It was a human soup. Nine hundred.

I prostrated for myself, for all these family members and even for all of humanity.

Bears, deer, bugs came next. Any creature, large or small, was added to my visualization, my prayers and my prostrations. One thousand.

I imagined purification and forgiveness and transcendence for everyone and only stopped because soon—very soon—the yurt would be needed for teachings.

Far off, in the lean-to kitchen, I heard the breakfast bell ring.

Twelve hundred!

WHY IN GOD'S name would anyone do these crazy prostrations? I wondered this to myself, as I sat down on my cushion and swabbed off the sweat and sucked for air. I wondered at the question for years in fact.

In part, I was desperate. I truly believed my only happiness would come from full enlightenment. And I did them because they were expected. Tylanni had done Ngondro as a young woman, and as a student of Tylanni—well, I wanted to be obedient. But there is more to the story—there usually is. In doing those prostrations, something incredible was also happening. I was pressing my forehead to earth, which is a form of frontal lobe therapy as was later explained to me by experts of the brain. It seems I was bowing to heal my own trauma.

WHEN YOU ARE a student of Rinpoche, you get to meet with the great master—one on one.

It's called semtri, or "pointing out instruction," where Rinpoche is able to see the nature of your mind. While I had no idea what this "nature of mind" meant, I was properly impressed. I had heard that a student could become enlightened during Sem Tre. Rinpoche could tell you one small thing and poof, enlightenment. Of course, I didn't know anyone this had happened to. It was like a Tibetan urban legend—useless but intimidating.

I WAS SHUTTLED up to Tylanni's house, which was at the top of a mountain, for my meeting.

I waited my turn in a small bedroom, sitting very still with my hands in my lap.

Although I would never admit it—I was too devoted to Tylanni to outwardly question this whole scene—I didn't know about being a student of Rinpoche's. He was thirty-four years old, a monk, and from Tibet. What did a young monk know about a divorced mother of two from America?

Across the spectrum of another possibility, I asked myself, What if he knew everything? What if Rinpoche—via his powers of enlightenment—could see so deeply in me that he'd view my past lives and my ruined karma, which were ripening in this life? Would he take one look into my eyes, shake his head, and send me away like some kind of all-knowing grim reaper? Would he say, "I am sorry Jennifer, but your next life will be lived as a bug. Bad karma. Baaad bad karma."

When it was finally my turn and I was being led into the room, I felt sure I was doomed.

Rinpoche was positioned on a loveseat that had been covered in maroon fabric.

The man was the size of an NFL football player. His shoulders were draped in maroon fabric. His head was shaved to less than a quarter inch of black stubble. His skin was dark brown.

Spencer, who had met Rinpoche on another retreat, said it like this: "When I met with Rinpoche, I felt like a fifty and when I was done talking to him, I felt like a thousand!"

It was true—to be in Rinpoche's presence could make a person happy. The man was enlightened after all, but aside from the whole enlightenment label, he was also a very cheerful person. He smiled a lot and had a huge belly laugh.

As I positioned myself on a mat on the floor, I bowed and trembled like a dashboard dog. How I longed for Spencer's optimism. He was blessed to be so open and so free.

Rinpoche's translator sat on a mat next to me. Her name was Anne and she was from Texas, a scholar at Rice University who devoted her adult life to translating the work of great Tibetan masters.

Next to her, I felt myself becoming that much more tiny and insignificant. Given my first inclination, I would have put my head down on the floor and cried. Instead, I just sat there and waited for my sentence—as if Rinpoche were my judge.

Afternoon sun fell through the western windows; its warmth spread across my back.

Anne told Rinpoche I had done twenty-five thousand prostrations and would be done with Ngondro right on schedule.

Rinpoche did the double thumbs up motion, which he had learned from his American friends. It was funny, that thumbs up, but I couldn't laugh. I couldn't even smile.

"Rinpoche is pleased," Anne said. "He says you are a very diligent, hard-working student."

Diligent? Hard working? Okay, this was a good beginning.

Rinpoche became serious and cleared his throat. He spoke in Tibetan and I flipped open my notepad. Anne leaned over and said I couldn't write.

In fact, our meeting was sacred and private. I was not to repeat anything—even the questions he would ask. My writing, my note pad and the little mechanical pencil I carried everywhere—my only devices of security—were gone. I had to rely on my mind, my memory, and my heart. Even though none of these had me failed me before, I lost all faith and became defined by fear.

Rinpoche asked a series of questions related to Buddhism and to meditation practice, things about Buddhist theory—of which I knew the answers—but he told me I couldn't respond. He said I needed to go think instead. He wanted me to come back with the answers later.

Did I mention I wanted to put my head down and cry?

I scurried out of our meeting, left Tylanni's house, and hiked down the treacherous mountain road as the heat of the day rolled sweat down my spine.

I needed to be away from witnesses and my teachers. I needed to go off alone and cry—yet again.

When I was a good distance away from the house and any possible spectators, I stopped walking and the let the tears fall. They weren't the monster tears of three years earlier—the Tara tears that constituted a lifetime of unknown grief. These were tears of defeat.

I READ A book once by an American man who claimed he had experienced the transcendent state—enlightenment. He wrote, "There were a few moments of apprehension as the Self died."

This Self, described as "dying," felt like an O-ring on the space shuttle—something that fell away when it was no longer needed and yet necessary for the initial lift-off into the nongravity state.

I underlined the passage and began to study the Self, which is defined as a complete and individual personality, especially one that somebody recognizes as her or her own and with which there is a sense of ease.

In Jungian theory, the Self is the totality of the psyche, the coherent whole symbolized by the circle (mandala), which pulls together the conscious and unconscious mind and integrates the personality.

I had to admit that I did not recognize my Self with a sense of ease. I did not feel that I had a solid container that held a coherent personality or a total psyche either. My dreams were filled with stories of being lost in buildings, taking wrong turns on unknown roads, missing flights, and losing my car. During the daylight hours, there was a lack of continuity in my thinking and even in my actions. I had a stop-start quality that I could not seem to control and this quality was tied to a bundle of complex and confusing emotions—primarily grief—but if I pushed to look more deeply, there was also a good share of anger too.

Initially, I believed my condition was the result of the many traumas of my past—the deaths, the sexual assaults, the terrors, the lies, and the betrayals. But I had examined all of these experiences with microscopic attention. I had written books, seen therapists, and studied. Certainly, through conscious attention to myself, I should have been able to heal; yet my inner Self wasn't intact, and I had proved this truth—once again—in the meeting with Rinpoche. I was—outside of my own control—tearing myself down.

Why?

What was wrong with me?

As I looked into the valley that held The Pure Land, tears rolled down my cheeks. I had seen into the nature of my own mind and knew I was not moving forward, despite my years of hard work. I was not strong enough to face apprehension, and even fear, and then pass through it. I was nowhere near the transcendent state. Being in service to The Pure Land and to Tylanni were not taking me where I needed to go either. Yet if Tylanni, these Buddhist teachings, and enlightenment weren't enough to bring me wholeness and peace, what else could there be?

The wind blew up the ridge and through the pine forest—the sound as big as a tidal wave. I faced the western sky, now ribboned with gold and pink light from the setting sun, and I had no answers to my own questions. Not one.

I pushed my tears away and continued down the rocky mountain trail, feeling weary beyond my years. All I wanted was to go home and be with my kids.

TWENTY

HOME, AT LAST

SPENCER AND JOSEPHINE played in the hot tub out back, and I was at my desk, reading and responding to emails. Busy work.

Jo cried, "Mom-meee."

I went to the open window, just steps from my desk, and leaned out. Jo was standing in the tub, pointing one long arm at Spencer. She wore only a pair of cupcake panties. Total little girl exposure with long legs, knobby knees, and a proudly exposed flat chest.

"He's splashing . . . " Jo began.

" . . . I didn't. I swear," Spencer interrupts. His expression held innocence.

"Why is she soaking wet?" I asked.

Jo was drenched, her face still dripping.

"Well, maybe a little bit . . . " he admitted.

While Spencer was caught off guard, she splashed him back.

Spencer sputtered, taking up the role of victim Jo had left behind.

"Did you see that? Did you see what she did?"

I just shook my head, rolling my eyes. These people were so crazy and funny.

"Please don't fight," I said. "I'll get into the tub with you guys in a second."

Spencer, outraged, did a huge splash back at Jo and the whole thing began again.

"MOM!" Jo yelled.

"Spencer! Enough! Both of you," I said. "I'm coming. Sixty seconds. Count so I can hear you."

They started counting, loud—one, two, three—and I sailed back to my desk to look at the last email, which was from an adoption organization in Virginia. It was an invitation to speak at their annual meeting. The author of the email had been trying to find me through my publisher and had just found my website.

"Ten, eleven, twelve," they counted.

I read and then reread the invitation.

Adoption? Why would I want to talk to anyone about adoption?

"Twenty-five, twenty-six . . . "

I typed fast: *I am not an expert on adoption. Many apologies. Good luck.*

I hit the send button and raced down the steps, pulling off my clothes as I went. Under my jeans and top, I wore a bathing suit—like some kind of super hero, ready for action! I tossed my clothes on a chair in the dining room and jogged out back.

"Sixty!" they both said at the same time.

Crisis averted.

I NO LONGER pushed myself to be in service to Tylanni or to travel the great distance to The Pure Land for retreats. It was just too exhausting and too expensive to live bisected between being Jennifer Lauck and Jampel Sherab.

I did continue my meditation practice, though. I had made a commitment to complete my Ngondro and I was not going to quit—no matter what.

I completed the practice right on schedule—done in the two years requested by Rinpoche—and savored the accomplishment in the solitude of my bedroom. On my last prostration, a poster of Tara fell down and broke across my altar. Water bowls tipped over, a crystal shattered, and I stood there—panting and sweating—while I stared at the impossible scene that marked prostration 108,000.

It was like some message from the gods or the deities or the higher forces of the universe. I thought, *I am not alone.* I had never been alone, not like I thought I had been, and this realization had me on my knees as if I had witnessed a miracle.

Ngondro had been my Mt. Everest, my Tour de France, my English Channel crossing. And I had done it. Moreover, I had done it and something bigger than me had said, "Yes, you did it!"

MY EVENING WITH the kids fell along the lines of our established routine—Jo, Spencer, and me. Play, homework, and dinner.

We clustered together on the sofa and I read *Judy Moody* to Jo and *Harry Potter* to Spencer. While I read, Spencer drew an excavation exhibition into a crystal cave far under the surface of the earth.

Jo drew princesses who held flowers in their outstretched hands. They continuously interrupted me to show off their creations and I told them how wonderful and talented they were. They both shimmered with the attention and the praise.

AFTER THE PHYSICAL exertion of Ngondro, I opted to take a quiet and relaxing Qi Gong class at a nearby college of natural medicine. Qi Gong was a welcome change to those damn prostrations but even more welcome was the teacher—a tall Midwestern man with red hair and a red beard. He was calm, peaceful, and fantastically beautiful. Now there was a man to rest your eyes on.

Upon closer inspection, I saw he was also married and that was just as well. I wasn't ready for a relationship—yet.

AFTER THE CHILDREN fell asleep, I went to my office to check my computer. A response had come from the Virginia adoption organization. The writer insisted that as an adoptee, I was the ideal speaker for their annual event.

Cricket song whined through the open window and the glow of the computer lit up my face in the darkened room.

The amount of money she offered was staggering. I thought, *You're a fool to pass up a paying gig, Jennifer!*

But adoption? What could I say that would mean anything? I knew nothing about adoption other than the fact that I had been adopted—twice—and in my own opinion, adoption was not a great choice. I also knew, given a preference, I would not adopt a child. No way. But these were my experiences and my opinions. They were not flushed out with any deep thought or consideration. Frankly, I didn't really want to think about adoption at all.

I sat in the dark of my office for a long time, considering my options.

IT TOOK A few weeks but I added up several hours of conversation with the directors, organizers, and promoters who worked with that Virginia adoption organization.

I tried to understand how I could contribute. I asked questions and conducted interviews. I discovered that none of the people who managed adoptions for this group had been adopted. None of them had experienced mother-loss of any sort either.

This seemed incredible. I would have thought that the first order of business for those who handled adoptions would be empathy garnered by direct experience. How can one know the power of mother-loss unless they too have lost a mother?

I was driven to read many books on adoption, B. J. Lifton's *Journey of the Adopted Self*, Jean Strauss's *Birthright*, Florence Fisher's *The Search for Anna Fisher*. I even called one of the authors, Nancy Verrier, who had written the books *Primal Wound* and *Coming Home to Self*.

Once I got Nancy Verrier on the phone—in a kind of informal interview—I asked what she would tell people if she were giving the talk. Nancy was quick to offer her own wisdom—garnered from years of working with adoptees, first mothers, and adoptive parents:

"Tell them to have empathy for the children in their care. They are grieving a terrible loss of the mother and of identity. Tell them to not expect gratitude from these children. They have no gratitude to give. Tell them to read my book and other books by experts."

As she spoke, I knew what I would say in Virginia. Her words became my speech.

When the interview was over, Nancy and I continued to talk. It turned out she was also a therapist, and after I had told her my personal story, she asked, "Have you ever explored the possibility of finding your birth mother?"

"No," I said, but then I stopped. I swallowed a lump that had formed in my throat. "Well, actually," I continued, "that's not true. I did search for her but that was a long time ago . . ."

TWENTY-ONE

FAVORITES

IN AN ODD TWIST OF FATE, the beautiful Midwestern Qi Gong instructor was not so married after all. In fact, he was in the midst of a divorce from a long-dead marriage. His children were grown. His wife was engaged to another man.

Amen!

I was bold. I told him to call me. "You know, if you want," I added, in order to show the proper respect.

He called right away.

A first date proved what I already knew. He was soft spoken, gentle, kind, and steady. A good man.

I didn't believe such a man would be possible for me. I just couldn't have imagined it, and yet, here he was.

Within a few weeks, he became a fixture in our lives.

His name was Roger.

Josephine called him Rogert. Spencer called him Rog. I called him Rogelio.

Rogelio was from Cleveland and was related to Kurt Vonnegut. He taught classic Chinese medicine and studied Tibetan Buddhism. He was a brilliant thinker with a doctorate in acupuncture. He was also fluent in many languages—Chinese, Portuguese, Spanish. When he spoke to me in Spanish, my knees went weak.

I was tentatively happy with Rogelio, sharing my children and our routine. He came to our house for time in the hot tub and dinners of mac and cheese. He danced in the kitchen with Jo and helped Spencer with his math homework. He talked to Steve with respect and Steve even said he liked him. "He's a different kind of dude," Steve said. "Isn't he?"

"Yes," I agreed. "He is a different kind of dude."

WHEN ROGELIO SAID he loved me, I was suspect. I told myself—as a ploy to undo the couple we were becoming—that we were doomed to bad timing. He had to manage the complexities of his divorce and I was deep in therapy with Nancy on the question of my own adoption, a process that was emotional and intense. We were digging into unexplored terrain that left me sad and often in a state of deep shock.

I told Rogelio, right up front, I believed myself too unstable for such a good man. "Just ask Steve," I advised.

Rogelio, not easily swayed, said he found me quite stable, thank you very much. He also volunteered to be part of a few telephone meetings with Nancy. He wanted to understand. He wanted to help.

Nancy told Roger that I would test him—try to push him

away—it was standard procedure for adoptees. "She has been abandoned by her mother at birth. It is a loss that goes deep."

Nancy encouraged Roger to read everything he could about adoption and to be prepared for a rocky ride, in the event I searched for my birth family.

"Reunions are very emotional," she warned. "Get ready."

I was sure the therapy with Nancy would be our breaking point but Rogelio said he wasn't going anywhere. He promised to stay at my side—no matter what.

ADOPTION BOOKS PILED up around my house and I read bits from each one. They contained testimonies, research, charts, data, and evidence. I talked to experts on the phone and combed the Internet.

As I moved closer to the idea of searching for my birth family, I felt hooked by an odd and binding loyalty to Bud and Janet. I told myself that to search would be a betrayal to their memory.

This belief expressed itself as a form of combativeness directed at Nancy. "What is the point of searching for my mother?" I demanded. "What will I gain?"

Nancy—ever patient—said I would gain an identity.

"I have an identity," I insisted. "I know who I am."

Nancy said no, I didn't know who I was and then she had me answer a series of questions.

Q: What is your favorite color?

A: I like lots of colors.

Q: What is your favorite food?

A: Oh, I like so many kinds of food.

Q: What's your favorite ice cream?

A: Well, sometimes I like mint chocolate chip but chocolate is good too. I don't know. I really don't have a favorite. I don't even like ice cream.

Q: What is your favorite tree, flower, book?

A: There is no way I could possibly choose. There are so many.

Q: Political affiliation?

A: None.

WHILE THIS WAS hardly a definitive test of identity, I found it odd I was so evasive. When it came to the children, I had no end of confidence. I could tell Nancy that Jo loved pink and Spencer loved Red. Jo's favorite food? Meatballs and mac and cheese. Spencer went for sushi, every single time. Jo loved cookie dough ice cream. Spencer only ate caramel swirl from Baskin-Robbins.

Yet I couldn't tell her what I would choose or what I would have chosen as a child.

I thought I struggled with a fragmented Self but Nancy was showing me that I actually lacked a Self. There was no "I" in "me" and her questions finally pinned me down and brought me face to face with the horrible truth.

I should have been relieved because finally there was someone in this world who could help me, but I wasn't. I was defensive and furious. I threw the stupid test in the garbage, but not before wadding it into a tiny, crumbled ball.

Nancy called this reaction progress.

She said we were getting to the heart of the matter.

My angry inner baby was finally showing herself.

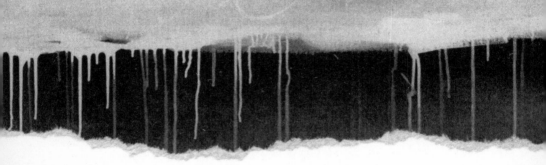

TWENTY-TWO

NEVER GIVE UP

THE LAST BLOCK to my search was my own desire to control the outcome of my own story. I felt I had to know all scenarios before launching a search.

1. My mother was dead.

2. My mother had been in a terrible accident and lost her memory.

3. My mother was alive and didn't want to know me.

4. My mother was alive and wanted to keep her past a secret.

5. My mother was alive and had been bullied into secrecy.

Nancy offered another version. "Very likely she is ashamed and scared."

"Well, that is pretty selfish," I said.

"Of course she is selfish," Nancy said. "What teenager isn't?"

"I don't get it," I said.

"She is likely trapped in the mindset of being seventeen. She is likely totally regressed. It happens. I see it all the time."

"But Nancy," I said, exasperated, "if my mother is someone

who did not have the courage to overcome these feelings put in place when she was a teen, how can I bear knowing her?' "

Nancy sighed on the phone—a sound I took to be impatience. I was sure all my questions wore her out but I didn't care. All my life I had been swayed by the will of another and I wouldn't be swayed by Nancy.

"Jennifer, you just need to meet your mother, have a cup of coffee, and talk," she said. "Meeting your mother is not about her personality. It's about the biology that connects you."

Nancy and I had been talking for months now. Fall had turned into winter and now it was spring. She had already told me these things over and over again but I couldn't seem to grasp the concepts.

She tried again—ever patient.

"It's as if you have put yourself on hold—from a sense perspective—from the moment you were born, and the only one who can take you off hold is your first mother," Nancy said. "She does this by being in the same room with you."

I opened my mouth to protest but before I could speak, Nancy continued.

"I know, I know, you are going to say I'm nuts but it's true. Human bonding is about the senses and you have not had your senses filled up by the mother who gestated you," she said. "You have been coping, Jennifer, and up to this point, you've been doing a remarkable job, but if you find her and spend some time in her presence, you will find your Self begin to take truer shape. You'll establish a firmer base than you've had—you will stop being so defensive and so afraid. You'll be able to move on. It's as simple as that."

Her words, as they always did, sparked tears. There was something in what she said that felt calming, as if there was a truth in the room. It also felt as if she were speaking to the deepest, most wounded part of myself—that baby that had yet to be fully born—the one I had been protecting since birth. But she was also speaking to the hardened survivor I had become. She was asking my protector to finally, fully step aside.

I just didn't know if I could do it. I had been protecting Jennifer for so long.

Back and forth I went for weeks and even months.

I was like a wild horse that wanted to sprint in the direction of my mother. I was also a magician who made the horse disappear by asking questions: *What if your heart gets broken? What if this woman hurts you again? What if? What if?*

BUT WHEN I finally decide to do something, anything, I give over my body, heart, mind to the job at hand. I become a laser beam of focus.

And that's what happened when I finally resolved to search for my first mother. Come what may, it became my job.

First, I hired an investigator who lived near Portland. Our work was on the Internet—a virtual investigation—and we spoke on the phone.

With nearly nothing to go on, the investigator pushed me to recover my copy of the Non-Identifying Information Report.

I told her it had been lost but I was pretty sure I threw it away after Bryan killed himself. I could almost see that old Jennifer wadding the page up and pitching it into the trash.

Goodbye, Mother. Good riddance, Dad.

Not to be thwarted, the investigator suggested I write Nevada for a copy. "Send a self-addressed, stamped envelope," she said. "It's your legal right to have that information."

I wrote the letter.

The state of Nevada is called a sealed state. This means it is the law to close adoption files. Not even a terminal illness can unlock them.

How odd that Nevada allows fast divorces and marriages and legalizes prostitution and gambling, but will not open adoption records.

The registry, established in 1979, remained active. I had called half a dozen times over the years, but stopped checking back before the kids were born.

When I wrote my letter to Nevada this time around, a response came right away: *No non-identifying information exists, sorry.*

I called the state and spoke to a woman named Angel and I thought it was a lucky sign. My name Lauck—luck with an A—was perhaps about to pay off.

As politely as possible, I suggested that Angel look in my file again. She did. No luck after all.

Still very polite, I asked if she was sure there was no non-identifying information because the state issued a document years ago and it had to be there. I felt like a mother chastising a child who had mislaid a toy. "It didn't grow legs and walk away, Angel. Go look again."

"I'm sorry, Ms. Lauck," Angel pushed back, "nothing is in this file except the name of your first mother."

A long, quiet ticking sound took over. My breath was gone.

"You have the name of my mother in front of you, right now?"

"That's right," she said, voice bright and even perky, "but I cannot tell you. That would be illegal."

It was as if Angel had struck me through the telephone line. I saw bright white light between my eyes.

"Do you know your mother, Angel?" I finally asked.

"Yes," she said, "I do."

"I'd like to know my mother too. Can't you tell me?"

"No, ma'am, I would lose my job."

She didn't hang up and neither did I. We breathed on the line— two women, two daughters, two human beings.

I imagined Angel in her Carson City office, sitting behind a big wooden desk. I saw her as a small woman with straight, dark brown hair. She had a pert nose and a slim, petite body. She dressed in conservative colors, gray, brown, black. Her nails were painted a clear color with little white bands at the top of the nail—French manicure. She had lived an entire life, luxuriating in a sense of self, forming a solid and impenetrable ego and now, she was unable to bend beyond rules written by a handful of old men more than a century ago. She likely thought this was some test, being conducted by a superior, and the excellent way she managed our conversation might lead to a promotion in the future.

Angel did not know me, nor did she care. I had no relevance to her life. I was a name, in a file, as was my mother.

LATER THAT SAME day, Spencer and I were in the car and on our way to Target. He juggled a thick wad of bills, saved from birthdays and allowance. The money was alive and he had to set it free. Target was the only store in town that carried the object of his desire—a mega-LEGO tech-tronic laser doohickey.

I was in no state to shop after my conversation with Angel. I needed to be on the sofa with a glass of wine and a bowl of extra perfect popcorn, my crazy comfort food—air-popped corn, melted butter, flax oil, salt, and a huge handful of Parmesan cheese. I needed to be watching a movie with the kids, letting them snuggle close while I numbed myself against the fact that someone else—a stranger—knew my mother. But there I was, being what I thought was a good mother.

Spencer chattered about the toy he wanted to get, with a LEGO magazine spread wide over his lap.

I nodded along with the cadence of his voice and kept my eyes on the six lanes of erratic traffic.

"What's going on, Mom?" he asked. "You seem different, kind of sad or something."

I made a lane change, checking my blind spot and just smiled.

"Nope, everything's fine. Just driving here."

Spencer reached over and touched my arm. "Come on, Mom," he said. "I can tell you are upset."'

I stopped at a red light and sighed.

Spence had a remarkable sensitivity to other people, especially me. Steve said no child should worry about a parent the way Spencer worried about me. "It's not healthy," he insisted.

With Steve's voice in my head, I adjusted the seatbelt strap and rolled my shoulders back. I tried to be reserved and cautious with Spencer. I certainly didn't want to screw up my child and I didn't want to burden him. I told Spencer a bit about the conversation with Angel.

"She had my mother's name, right there, and wouldn't tell me."

"Why not?"

"It's the law," I said.

"Well, that's a bullshit law!"

"Spence!" I said. "You owe me a quarter."

"Fine," he said, digging into his pocket and putting two quarters in the cup holder between us. "It's a totally bullshit law."

"Spencer!"

"I paid in advance, Mom. I bought that word."

I held the steering wheel with both hands, shaking my head and just imagining Steve's disapproval at the loose way I was raising our boy.

"Well, fine, it is a bullshit law," I said, passing him one of his quarters back.

Spencer grinned. He pocketed the quarter again.

The light changed and the driver behind me honked. I waved into the mirror and went through the intersection.

Spencer watched me and I smiled over at him.

"It just took the wind out of me, you know, like when you get body-checked in Tae Kwan Do? Maybe I'm never going to find my first mother. Maybe I should just quit."

Spencer nodded like yes, indeed he did know. Body blows were the worst, in his book. He cleared his throat then and spoke to me directly, with great earnestness.

"Master Dan says it's normal to get sad, Mom," he said, "but he also says to never give up."

Master Dan was Spencer's Tae Kwan Do teacher, a little Nepalese man wired as tight as a snare drum. I could hear his lilting Asian accent, "You, Spencer. You never give up! Okay? Never give up!"

My boy had turned the tables on me. He was giving me advice with my own example.

I took up his other quarter and gave it back too.

"You're going to need that for your Legomegawhozit," I said.

Spencer laughed and took the quarter, shoving it into his front pocket. He looked at his magazine again, making his plans, and I moved my hand over the back of his head—one of his favorite things. I had been touching him that way since the day he was born. He smiled a little secret smile.

"You're a great kid," I said.

"You're a great mom," he said.

MY INVESTIGATOR HAD me register on something called the online bulletin boards, Internet sights where adoptees and birth parents placed posts.

"Looking for a young man born around Feb. 8, 1976, his birth name was——. Please, if anyone knows anything please let me know."

"MY NAME IS——, I'M SEARCHING FOR MY BIRTH

FAMILY I WAS BORN IN LAS VEGAS, NEVADA AT SUN-
RISE HOSPITAL ON FEBUARY 6, 1968, AT 8:26 AM."

"My son, born Feb. 8, 1976, Elko, Nevada. Welfare took him
away, please tell him I love him and never stop thinking of him."

Reading these online postings was like being at the sight of a
great tragedy where people wandered in a daze as they called out
the names of missing loved ones. It felt like futility to add my own
information. I was sure if my mother didn't register to find me in her
own state, she was not out here surfing obscure Internet sites. But I
added my information anyway—just in case.

The next idea was to write to the Reno High Alumni Association. Very likely, according to my investigator, my mother had been
a student there. She said girls didn't usually have babies in towns like
Reno. Most often they were sent away to places like San Francisco or
Los Angeles.

I found the Reno High Alumni Association online and wrote to
every registered member. I attached a photo of myself.

Several graduates wrote back. Names like Donna, Lanette,
Lenda, Linda, Ruby, and Alice passed through my email account.
They all wrote the same thing: *So many girls were pregnant during
those years. It was all so hush-hush. It was better to be a murderer than to
be pregnant.*

I was given several names and with the help of the investigator,
I found each woman.

When I called these women, my hands shook and my heart
caught a beat. I was potentially about to meet my mother. I had to

remind myself that I had been a reporter who once interviewed murderers, beauty queens, and even presidential candidates. If I did all that, I could ask a stranger if she was my mother.

Not one of the women turned out to be the one.

All of them were very gracious, apologetic, and even hopeful. One woman, who gave up her son when she was sixteen, offered to be my mother. "You seem so nice," she said. I asked why she hadn't searched for him yet, and she became very quiet. "Oh, I couldn't do that," she said. "I don't want to upset his life."

FOUR MONTHS PASSED with no success when Aunt Georgia, a long-lost relative from the past who lived in Carson City, told me—in an offhand conversation about my search—that I needed to contact Catholic Community Services.

She insisted this organization had my non-identifying information.

Georgia, the wife of Janet's brother, Uncle Charles, had long been a true angel in my life. She had been the reason Bryan and I were saved from L.A. and Deb, but over the years—especially after my divorce from Steve—we had lost touch.

And I felt guilty telling her about the search for my birth mother. I didn't want to insult Janet's memory or her relatives by suggesting I might need more than the memory of a dead woman. I knew Aunt Georgia came from the old school of people who said things like: "Adoption means nothing. You were loved and that's all that matters."

While Aunt Georgia didn't understand my need to search and couldn't raise the empathy to encourage me forward, she did make a point of telling me to look in the right place. "I'm telling you it was Catholic Charities that managed your adoption. Not the state."

A FEW DAYS later, an email came in from Catholic Community Services of Northern Nevada.

The email began: "Dear Jennifer, Thank you for writing and yes, indeed, your adoption was facilitated by our organization . . . "

I sat back in my chair, my hand over my mouth.

It was an ordinary day—another fall day—the leaves on the red oak were turning yellow again.

Aunt Georgia had been right.

The email went on to say a file was in their office and that I needed to send a certified letter to request a copy of the Non-Identifying Information Report.

I typed a message back to the organization. I wrote that a certified letter would go out immediately.

TWENTY-THREE

FOUND

MY MOTHER HAS BEEN FOUND. She lives in Reno, Nevada. Her name is Catherine.

Catherine, Catherine, Catherine.

How did I know?

Within one hour of receiving the Non-Identifying Information Report from Catholic Community Services, my investigator unearths Catherine's birth records, marriage records, and even a couple divorces. She lives in Reno and has been there—a few miles from St. Mary's Hospital—nearly all of her life.

Knowing she is out there and has been there all this time becomes such a blow, I have to bend over to catch my breath.

Knowing she has been found also sets me into a shaking fit of urgency as if I will burst from my skin. *I must get to her.*

In order not to explode or pull myself apart, I concentrate all my energy into a calm, unemotional focus that is a bit frightening to observe from the outside. It's like being in a newsroom, listening to police scanners and picking out the tragedies that will lead the evening report—Murder? Drug bust? Massive pileup on the interstate? As a reporter, I didn't let myself feel the sorrow that came with such tragic events and I do not let myself feel anything now.

Calculating. That's what I become. I am streamlined calculation.

I determine that my first contact with Catherine will not happen near my children or Rogelio. Complete silence is what I require to maintain focus and to hold steady.

As I drive through town, navigating through traffic, I must ask myself, Why I am hardening in this way? What am I afraid of?

I cross the Willamette River via the steel bridge and sunlight shines on the surface of the water. A few kayaks are out, drawing ripples on the surface of the river.

The answer to my question is obvious. I am terrified she will reject me, yet again.

I pull into the parking lot of my office, pop the trunk, and unload the back of the car. The world goes on around me—birds singing, wind blowing, sun shining—and I carry all my equipment up the stairs and juggle out the keys that open the front door.

Crazy spaghetti western movie music plays in my head—that whistling dusty tune—and I feel like Clint Eastwood with a dirty five o'clock shadow and spurs on my boots. All I need is a ragged wool poncho and a couple guns in my holsters.

As I go inside, I know I am preparing myself for a showdown with the mother who never searched. I am getting ready to hear the truth, even if it includes, "Go away. I don't want to remember."

MY OFFICE IS a lot like a favorite living room might be—a dream space with overstuffed furniture covered in velvets and silks. Fresh flowers are on a low pewter table and pillows are scattered around. My desk, from France, is hand painted and overhead is a chandelier of draping crystals and sweeping brass.

Josephine calls my office the Princess Palace. To her eyes, it's a fairy wonderland for a little girl who still believes in magic.

Did I ever believe?

Before living with Jo, I'd say no.

After seven years of being her mother and having access to her way of thinking and living, I'd call myself a full convert.

But as I turn on the overhead light, setting the chandelier on dim, I forget all that Jo has taught me. I lose track of the power of fairies and dreams and magic. I am again, once again, governed by fear.

One thing I finally possess, though, is certainty.

I am certain I will not leave this office until I have made contact with Catherine.

I UNPACK MY files, computer, and telephone. I unwind my power cords, get a wireless signal, and put my phone on the charger.

As command central comes to life, an email beeps into my account. It is a message from my investigator. She has typed Catherine's phone number in large, bold text. *I'm sure you're overwhelmed right now,* she writes. *I can't wait to hear when you make contact.*

I squint at the numbers on the screen, pick up the phone, and dial.

Catherine's number rings several times and then a series of clicks send the call to her answering machine. A woman's voice says, "No one is in to take your call. Leave a number and we'll call you right back."

Is it her?

The *t*'s and *k*'s are clipped and quick, in the same way I clip my own *t*'s and my *k*'s, and my tough-guy façade shifts—just a little—like a poncho sliding off my shoulders.

Jesus—my voice.

I'm a wicked mimic of other people but I have never heard my own voice coming back at me.

I barely pull myself together to leave a message, which is short and odd—I think I leave a name and ask that she call me.

After I hang up, I imagine Catherine listening to my message, screwing up her face with the question—*What? Who the hell is this?* I see her hit the erase button and continue on with her life.

I hit re-dial on my phone and her machine picks up again. After the beep, I speak with more authority: "This is Jennifer Lauck, again. I need to leave a little more information . . ."

When I am done, I do not press the off button or close the phone. I exist in the silence of the open line as if she were standing right there, listening, and might just pick up.

The investigator sends one, two, three, and then five more emails. They come in a fast sequence and each holds more information, lists of telephone numbers for those related to Catherine—brothers, a sister, an ex-husband, friends, and her kids. This is when I discover my father's full name too. William Wright.

I tug out a high school yearbook from Reno High (sent by a member of the alumni association). I scan through the photos from 1961 and there they are. Catherine and Bill.

Bill is a dark, moody-looking guy who tucks his chin in the photo as if he wants the photographer to go away. Dad?

Catherine is—simply put—stunning. Model beautiful. Luminous skin. Shining blond hair and a delicate face and—my God— she looks just like Jo.

Looking at her photo weakens me. My mother. She looks so fragile and beautiful and exactly as she should look.

Catherine kills me without even being in the room.

SOME MIGHT QUESTION why I didn't wait awhile and let Catherine call me back. Some might say, "Geez, what's the hurry? Give the woman a chance."

To really understand the intensity of my own desire is to go back to karma, cause and effect, and even Newton's Law of Motion, which states: *For every action, there is an equal and opposite reaction.*

I was now getting very close to someone who had never searched for me and had potentially locked me away—as a deep secret. To bury something as powerful as life, which includes identity and self-hood, is to beg for it to explode to the surface. I am motivated, very likely, by the very power of the polarized system in which I exist. I am reaching for the light of my truth. One more moment of being suppressed is unbearable to me.

It isn't me that creates the condition of urgency. It is actually Catherine, by her denial of me, who provides much of the momentum.

I PLAY A little game of roulette. I spin the names sent by my investigator and make a random choice.

I decide to call a guy named Darrell. He's a cousin. I find his photo on the Internet. He sells real estate. He's a broker. We part our hair to the side, in the exact same way. He has sad eyes and a nice smile. Darrell looks like a good man.

A receptionist says Darrell is in a meeting and sends my call to voice messaging. His voice also has the familiar twang I recognized in Catherine. I leave a message that is, at best, cryptic.

I go through the list again and pick another name. It is a thirty-six-year-old woman who shares a name with Catherine. A daughter?

"Hello?" the woman says on the phone.

I pause at the sound of an actual human being. I clear my throat and ask if she is related to Catherine.

"I am," she says. "She's my mother. Who is this?"

I want to put the phone down and lay on the floor, panting from the effort it has taken to get this far.

"I think she's my mother too," I make myself say.

"What?"

"Go to your computer, if you have one—"

"I have one," she says. "I'm there."

It's too fast, she moves too quickly, but her speed is also perfect. She has to be my sister.

I ask for her email address and she gives it without hesitation. I send photos of myself, and after a second, hear the beep of an email arriving on her end.

"Oh my God," she finally says. "Is this you?"

"Yes," I say. "I hope I'm not freaking you out."

"You are totally freaking me out," she says. "Wow!"

Her voice pattern is like mine, not exactly the same, but so close and again, I am undone.

Her name is Jessica but she says she goes by Jessie. She has a young voice with a familiar cadence. It's not like Catherine's voice on the answering machine, but I feel the nuances that make her voice and diction like my own.

"You really look like us," Jessie says, as she looks at the photos online. It's almost as if she has been waiting for something like this. She is that fast to process and to speak.

"My mom did marry a guy named Bill, just after high school. They had my brother Daniel but then they got divorced and she married my father and oh my God, your dad, Bill, he died a couple years ago, I think. I heard he died anyway. Oh my God, I'm so sorry to tell you that but I guess you should know."

I am so into her inflections and tones that I'm not fully hearing what she says. Her words glance off me, unable to penetrate. Did she say my mother married my father? That I have a brother—a one-hundred-percent brother? Did she say my father is dead?

"I'm your sister," Jessie says.

We both laugh, in the same way, at the same tempo.

"Do you know where she is?" I ask. My voice is small and hopeful.

"At work, I just talked to her like an hour ago," she says. "I talk to her every day, sometimes three times a day."

A sting enters my body and catches my breath. She talks to her mother every day, three times a day?

"We tell each other everything," Jessie says. "I thought I knew everything about her . . . "

Her voice trails away.

Both of us are lost now. Both of our realities are changing. Both of us must manage our own sense of betrayal.

"I'm truly sorry," I say. "I hope I haven't upset you."

"No, it's okay. I'm just so surprised," she says.

"I get it, and you know what—I just want to find my mother."

"Of course you do," she says. Her immediate understanding catches me by surprise. I expected resistance and even doubt but not this. If I had been looking for a sister, I might slow down a little and let myself linger on what we have stumbled upon, but I am a heat-sinking missile of focus again—I just want the person who has denied me all these years. I want my mother.

"Can you do me a favor and call your mother? Can you break the news in a gentle way? Can you let her know I'm here and want to talk to her, tonight, as soon as possible? Can you tell her I don't want to make any trouble? I just want to talk, that's all."

"Our mother," Jessie interrupts.

"What?"

"She's our mother," she insists. "You are just going to have to get used to saying that."

When Jessie calls again, she says Catherine is frantic.

"She had to leave work. She was sobbing and hysterical. She's upset and confused. I'm sure you understand," Jessie says.

"Of course," I say.

"She says she knew about you. She saw that email that you sent to the Reno High alumni, like a couple months back?" she asks. "Is that right?"

"I did," I say. "I sent a photo too. She saw it?"

"She thought your message was a hoax and she deleted it."

"She deleted me?"

Jessie says nothing. How terrible it must be for her to tell me— the first born—such a shocking thing. *You were deleted.*

Jessie finally says she's sorry about all this, as if she wants to make up for what is going down. But I know she is innocent. This mess is not her doing or her job to clean up.

I'm not mad at Jessie, not in the least.

I clear my throat and refocus. "Can she call me?"

"I told her to," Jessie says, "but she is really torn up about this. She didn't want anyone to know and now she's going home to call my brother, my father, her own brothers and sister and several friends. She says she needs to let everyone know her secret before they find out. That's the way she is. She worries they will all hate her. You understand all this, right?"

"Of course," I manage to say but the fact that my mother is not calling me first makes me ache. I feel pain in my head, at the base of my neck, and the core of my body goes ice cold. The world feels surreal. It's like a bad dream.

"I'll do my best to have her call," Jessie says, "I promise."

When she hangs up, I pull a blanket off the sofa. I wrap myself tight. I chant Tara, I pray to Mary, I ask God—whatever that force of energy is, to give me strength. I rock forward and back—alone.

An hour passes and finally the telephone rings again.

I drop the blanket and snap the phone open.

"Jennifer?" comes a delicate voice.

"Yes," I manage to say.

"This is your mother," my mother's voice is weak and broken, a frail warbling. "I want you to know not a day has gone by that I haven't thought about you."

Like an old dog, tired to the marrow, I cannot respond to what she says. I can only lie down on the floor of my office, pull my knees close to my chest, fetal, and close my eyes.

Catherine goes on to tell her story. It spills from her almost like a prepared script.

She says she was just seventeen years old, crazy in love with Bill, a boy her mother did not approve of. "I remember saying, 'But mom, we're in love. I love him.' My mother told me to knock it off."

Catherine sounds like she is crying.

"My mother, your grandmother, she had a good heart. She meant well," she says. "She died a couple years ago. Today is actually the anniversary of her death. I just realized that."

"I'm sorry," I manage to say. *I'm sorry? Is that true?*

"Thank you," Catherine says. "I really miss her. Every day I feel like crying. She was my whole life."

There are two Jennifers now. One of us dissolves back to the beginning of herself and she is a baby again. The details Catherine speaks of don't matter, my mother is here and the sound of the voice matches a pattern I've been waiting for since the day I was born. All is well. But there is also "survivor Jennifer," who wants to tell Catherine that she knows full well what it is to miss a mother. Survivor Jennifer wants to pick a fight. Who does this woman think she is? Who does she think she is talking to?

Catherine, oblivious to these divided portions of Self, goes on to say she wanted to be with my father more than anything in the world but since she was so young—the whole thing was out of her hands.

She says she can't really remember her pregnancy at all. "Isn't that funny?" she asks.

I want to say, "No, that is not funny, it is tragic."

I say nothing.

"And I don't remember having you either," she continues. "I just remember going into the hospital, being drugged, having a doctor come in, take you out, and then you were gone."

I weep now, tears falling on the rug.

"I never even got to hold you," Catherine says, "but my mother did get to see you. She told me you were beautiful with a bunch of dark hair. And that was it. Whenever I thought about you or even about looking for you, my mother would tell me, 'Forget it, she has her own life. She's happy. You're just going to mess things up.'"

Finally, Catherine goes silent. The wind blows outside and the branch of a rhododendron bush scrapes against the window.

I realize I have been here, in my office, for six hours.

It feels like a moment.

It feels like forever.

I push myself off the floor, wipe the tears from my face, and move to the sofa where I ease into a nest of velvet pillows.

I know this is my chance to say something and I search for words. I want to speak the truest truth but what is the truth?

It's Catherine who speaks once again. "So," she says, as casual as if meeting me on the street. "How have *you* been?"

This is such a funny question and we both laugh in the same way, at the same tempo.

The release of seriousness is a relief and within, I feel a rise of love so pure and so utterly familiar. It is the same feeling I have for my children, which began sprouting the moment I knew I was pregnant with them. When each child was placed in my arms, I was a goner. I know I have been waiting—for my true mother, for Catherine—in order to finally release this universal love in the other direction. Love has always been in my heart, waiting for the right person to trip the code.

I ONCE HEARD the Dalai Lama say, and I am paraphrasing, that after birth, our first experience is a mother's affection. A child may not have the idea "This is my mother," but there will be a connection because of the biological system. On the mother's side there is also that sort of tremendous feeling of care. He said this was not due to religious faith, but because of the biological factor. According to the great master, human bonding is the key that brings the deepest satisfaction to the world, it is the basis of our life breath and how our life started.

But what of the adopted child deprived of her mother? What of the birth mother deprived of her child?

Of course, I already knew the answer to these questions from my own experience. I also knew that love had been trying to find a way through me as I loved my own children and they loved me in return. Love was a force greater than political, cultural, and religious interventions. Love was bigger than this institution we called adoption. And love had more work to do in me. It had driven me to be on the phone, right now. I didn't have to defend or protect myself anymore. With my mother on the line, my good heart knew what to do.

I cleared my throat and spoke that truth.

"Thank you," I said. "Thank you for my life."

Catherine exploded like a heavy sky, tears raining, and her voice comes ragged.

"That is the most amazing thing you could have ever said to me," she managed. "I was just so sure you have hated me for what I did to you."

TWENTY-FOUR

CATHERINE

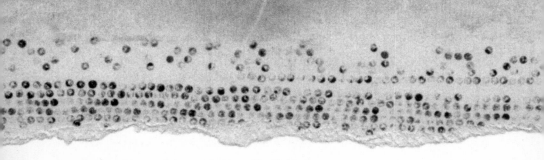

CATHERINE IS ON the earliest flight from Reno.

She will land in Portland by 8:00 AM.

I am going to pick her up at the airport.

We get a day together—just this day. She has a sick cat, a job that needs her, and appointments in her datebook she cannot possibly reschedule.

I STAND IN my closet and evaluate my wardrobe—jeans, tops, sweaters, skirts. What to wear? What to wear? Should I choose a fancy combination that makes me look pretty or perhaps something professional that makes me appear credible? Perhaps I can pick an ensemble that says, "Love me. Take me home with you. Don't leave me again."

CATHERINE AND I have talked, several times, on the phone. We've exchanged emails with photos from her life—Christmas holidays, anniversaries, birthdays, and graduations. In her pictures, I've seen aunts, uncles, a grandmother, and a brother and sister. My people. They all have the shape of my smile, the curve of my eyes, the size of my chin, and the span of my forehead.

As I look at the life my mother has gone on to have without me, I tell myself this story: *She had a decent life with family who loved her. That's good. I'm happy for her.*

Deep in me, though, pushed low and flat, another story rises. I finally feel what Catherine worried I would feel—a seething rage that turns the contents of my stomach to toxic waste. *She made a life without me. She made a life as if I didn't exist. She kept me a secret for forty-four years. She has even told me she would have never searched. Never!*

To cope with the pain I have been feeling for most of my life and have been denying and redirecting, I drink way too much wine late at night. Or, I get my bike out of the garage, pedal hard, and sweat myself blind as if in training for the Iron Man competition. Or, I press Spencer and Jo to my sides and read silly books like *Captain Underpants* and *Bad Kitty*. The latter is the only way to actually still the fury. Warm bodies, sweet breath, steady hearts, and the familiar sound of their laughter. They are whole and loved and kept children. Their proximity makes me whole and loved too—for a while.

BEIGE CORDS AND a black cardigan. I pull myself together in these clothes because they are everyday attire. Comfortable. After I am dressed and ready, I make a top-down survey in the full-length mirror.

There I am—Jennifer Lauck. I have long dark hair, deep dark eyes, a narrow face, and a slim form. My sweater is pilled and has a hole under the arm. My pants have a ripped pocket. I don't care.

I don't need to impress Catherine. Meeting her isn't a contest or a job interview.

In the main terminal of Portland International Airport, I am surrounded by a stream of travelers—arriving and departing.

I hold a bundle of roses cut from my back yard. They are the best of the year, buds the size of extra-large eggs. I've added sprigs of rosemary and lavender. The arrangement is wrapped in a white silk scarf.

This is a perfect demonstration of the kaleidoscope of conflicting emotion within. I hate the mother who gave me away. I love her enough to bring her the best from my garden. Hate and love work inside my skin—a tug of war between primal survival habits and the call of a higher consciousness. It's a miracle I am functioning at all.

At the inbound waiting area, I sit.

I check the time on my cell phone and then I check the time on my watch. There is a five-minute difference between the watch and the phone. I readjust the time on the watch.

Inbound travelers fill the corridor, people with busy expressions and quick strides. A businesswoman pulls a wheelie travel bag and talks on the telephone. Another woman, with a baby in a stroller, goes by. Next is a teenager listening to his iPod—jeans around his hips.

I shift to the edge of my seat.

Did she change her mind? Was her flight delayed?

I check my phone. No message.

A tall woman in high heels walks my way. She's wavy in my field of vision, like a mirage in the desert.

I stand up.

The woman wears open-toed strappy heels and slim-fitting jeans. She has narrow hips, a lean body, and wide shoulders she rolls back with the stance of a trained dancer. She has high, round cheekbones and her hair is a lovely shade of auburn.

"Jennifer?" she asks.

I nod. I think I nod.

We embrace but it's not like a hug, it's more like a magnetic slap against her body and on pure instinct, my arms go around her back, my chin digs into her collarbone, and I inhale the smell of her almond perfume. A flood of primitive relief moves through me. This is my mother. She is the one.

Catherine is more restrained. Her side of the embrace is brief and stiff. I've heard it is that way when the first mother has been found—they feel exposed and embarrassed. She has lived all my life, and most of hers, in shame and secrecy.

She is the first to break away.

While I make a mental note to give her room, an arms length is all I can allow. I keep my hand on her shoulder and feel the shape of her bones and even the texture of her muscles and skin through the fabric of her silky blouse. My mother is utterly familiar—like a dream I've been having all my life.

I regress as if I am one of my own children when they are in proximity to my body. I assume ownership of this stranger, my mother.

"My God, you are amazing," I hear myself say. "Look at you."

I take her in from the top of short auburn curls down to her toes painted a shining red. I touch her arms, to her elbows and wind my fingers into hers. "Do you play music?" I ask.

"No, no," she laughs.

I touch her hips. I turn her right to left and then left to right. I go around her, full circle—one way and then the other. "Look at your fucking legs," I say. "They are so incredibly long."

She laughs out loud.

"Look at your fucking legs," she says. She does this flashy gesture, opening her hands like a game show hostess.

I look at my own hands, which are just like hers and I see them in a new way. I have my mother's hands.

"How tall are you?" she asks.

"Five nine."

"I'm five ten," she says.

She holds out her foot. "What size are your feet?" she asks.

"I'm a nine," I say, kicking my foot out of my sandal.

"Me too," she says.

We laugh as if our shoe size is hilarious.

I TAKE CATHERINE to breakfast. A pancake and coffee place called Zells. We order the same thing, eggs on toast. While we eat, we talk fast. My words spill over hers and her words spill over mine. We are the same that way. We are talkers.

We drink cup after cup of coffee, reaching for the cream at the same time and then crack up when our hands collide.

We use our hands when we talk. We make windmill-sized gestures to get our points across. Our voices rise and then fall in the same vocal range.

Catherine and I are so alike—after a while, I cannot track the similarities.

WHEN WE HAVE wiped our mouths with our napkins and our plates are cleared, Catherine reaches into her purse and takes out a photo. She places it on the table between us—as if relieved to unburden herself. "It's the only photo I have of him," she says. "It's not very good."

The photo of my father is on a large sheet of color copy paper and he wears a military uniform. He poses next to a cannon six times larger than he is. He looks like a child playing dress-up in a grown man's clothes.

"I don't know a lot. We were just kids. I know his mother was divorced. She moved around a lot. I didn't really know her. She was called, what? A barfly? I don't think they were close."

Catherine searches over my head, as if more memories live there. "Um, he came back to Reno not long after you were born—we kind of fell back in together. Eloped when I got out of high school. I got pregnant on our honeymoon. After that, he was stationed in Germany. I had our son. It was a bad marriage. I missed my family. I left him in Germany and came back to Reno with the baby. I never saw him again. I wish I could tell you more. You know he's dead now?"

"Yes," I say, "I heard."

Catherine shrugs her pretty shoulders. She seems uncomfortable, even embarrassed as she delves into the past.

I study the photo of my father with more intensity but also find myself taking sides with Catherine. I feel embarrassed too, as if it's wrong to want to know him.

Catherine reaches to tuck a loose strand of hair behind my ear.

"I can't get over being here, together," she says. Her voice is different, soft and a little sad. "I've missed your whole life."

She drops her hand into her lap. Questions I may have about my father vanish and there is just the touch of mother. It was so fast, I wonder if it even happened. Did I make it all up?

Sometimes, when I stroke Spencer in a casual way—running my hand over the shape of his head or rubbing his back—and then stop, he'll take my hand and put it back on his body. It's his way of saying, "Keep touching me, Mom."

I want to take Catherine's hand and have her touch me again but I don't. I am too shy.

WE LEAVE THE restaurant and go to a house that has been offered by a friend. The kitchen has been stocked with cheese, fruit, bread, chocolate, wine, and teas.

Catherine and I spend our day on the back deck, surrounded by vines and passionflowers. We drink pots of tea and eat dark chocolate in the September sun. She likes dark chocolate as much as I do.

We perform an awkward dance of togetherness with steps we don't know how to execute. If I were a baby, I'd be naked in her arms and she'd touch me everywhere. She'd count my toes and press her face into my belly. But I'm a grown woman and neither of us knows how this is supposed to be. The threat of intimacy between us is overwhelming and intoxicating. She holds my hand for a long time and then, without warning, pulls back and crosses her arms over herself. I lean into her, closing my eyes to take in the sound of her voice and then scoot away, a twist of queasiness in my stomach.

"Do you want to see my photos?" I ask. A thick manila file holds images that go back to infancy.

"I want to see everything," she says.

I move through my life story with a casual swiftness, using each photo as a marker on the timeline. I can't linger on the losses or the pain or the loneliness. I want my mother to see the good things, the accomplishments and the success. I sit close to her while she looks at younger and still younger versions of me.

"This is me in high school," I say. "Can you believe the size of my nose?"

"You have your father's nose," she says.

"Really?"

"It suits you," she says. "I like it."

I am down to two photos, baby pictures. Both are of Janet holding me.

In the first, she poses in front of our little ranch house on Mary Street in Carson City. I'm swaddled in blue and yellow and have a bonnet on my head. Janet wears a matching outfit with a big yellow hat tilted at a jaunty angle.

Catherine removes her glasses and looks at the picture as if trying to find a way to pass through and go back in time.

"She's not holding you close enough," Catherine finally says. "What's wrong with her? I thought she was a mother already?"

I don't answer.

During my work with Nancy, I learned that Janet's attempts at closeness were rejected by me—as a part of my biological code. Janet didn't pass the sensory tests of sound, smell, and touch. In the photo, I'm being what is called a "stiff-armed baby." She's not pushing me away. I'm pushing her away.

How can I tell this to Catherine and not hurt her?

Catherine looks up and I silently pass her the next photo.

She makes another sound of disgust. "Why isn't she holding you closer?"

A stab of anger flashes, a bolt of lightening on a dry, hot night. I want to say, "Where were you? Why didn't you come?"

But I can't form the words. I don't want to be angry.

THE SUN ARCS over the house and a squirrel leaps from branch to branch on an old maple tree.

My photos are fanned out on the patio table. She holds the ones of me as a baby and studies each one for such a long time.

When Catherine finally speaks again, her voice is so low I have to lean closer still.

"I don't remember going into labor at all. I don't even remember that much about being pregnant with you, but I do remember being in the hospital. I was lying down. There was a doctor with a mask on his face. He just came in, took you out, and that was it.

"I think I looked up," she continues. "I wanted to see you but someone pushed me down again." She presses against her own shoulder, as if to remind herself of that moment and what happened. Her hand drops to her lap. "Then you were gone and I was taken to another part of the hospital where there were no babies. I was put into a room with an older woman who had been recovering from some surgery. She asked, 'What are you in for, Honey?' like I was in prison.

"I told her I didn't feel well," she says. "That's when the lies began."

She looks at me as if I could or should understand and I suppose I do. I want to understand.

"I went home and the birth was never mentioned again," she said. "I was so depressed. I kept getting lower and lower. My family was watching me all the time. Maybe they thought I would kill myself?"

She looks at me with the question, as if I have the answer.

I can only shrug and shake my head.

"When they finally left me alone in the house, I kicked the screen out of my window and walked to a mental hospital. A nice Indian doctor took me into a room and I talked about being depressed."

"Did you tell him you had a baby?" I interrupt.

She shakes her head. "I just told him I was depressed and he gave me some lithium. I threw away the pills and went home. I never got caught for sneaking out and I never told my mother."

She lays the photo of my infant self on the table and leans back. Her face is sallow. Her lips are curved down. The beautiful and confident woman at the airport and at breakfast has slipped away and the true Catherine is here—tormented, confused, and angry.

"If I ever asked about you and how you were, my mother would tell me to forget the whole thing. She told me no good could come from thinking about you. When I thought I might search for you, my mother told me I would just mess up your life and to let it go."

The sun is bright in her hair now, making it shine all different shades of reddish-brown. She looks so tired and so sad.

"I think about that," she says. "Why didn't I just search for you anyway? Why didn't I defy her? I went against her wishes other times. I married Bill right out of high school. I got pregnant and went to Germany with him after he was drafted. All of that was pure defiance. Why didn't I defy her when it came to you?"

"Did you ever talk about me while you were married to Bill?" I ask. My question sounds so small and pathetic as it emerges. I feel so needy. I cross my arms over my stomach, as if to hold on and comfort myself.

"I don't think so," she says. "Bill said we would make more children—lots of babies—and I just put the past in the past."

She waves her hand as if dusting something off the side of her neck and smiles her pretty smile. It seems so easy for her, so effortless.

A robin drops from the tree and lands on the fence. The color of his plumage is a rust and sable brown. The bird regards us with a tilt to his head, a shine in his small black eyes.

I cannot fathom how she went on to marry my father and how they had a son, who they kept, just three years after my own birth. I cannot understand how they didn't talk about me—at all.

How do I not take it personally? How do I not make a leap and say it must have been *me*—that I was lacking or worthless in some essential way? How do I overcome these feelings of lack in order to find my true human value when my own mother placed no value on my presence in the world?

I know I cannot ask her these questions. She is just too damn wounded and to ask that she help me sort things out—when she cannot even sort herself out—is impossible. It's a formula for failure. Or perhaps it is me who is too wounded. I have learned, early on, to hate myself for being needy and wanting to be wanted. I have cut those aspects of my personality away, in order to survive. And I do it again, as I sit here with Catherine. I tell myself to be stronger and get over it.

The bird does a small stutter step on the edge of the fence and drops into the neighbor's yard.

"You can have those baby pictures," I hear myself say. "I don't need them."

"Oh, that would be wonderful," Catherine says. She stacks the photos in a little pile and tucks them into her purse.

If a mother's welcoming embrace is the core to human satisfaction, then the rejection of a mother must be the root of human dissatisfaction. I am wholly dissatisfied at this moment. I feel as if my life has no value—none at all and I want so much to take her to the airport and go find my children as fast as I can. I want to go home to a steady source of original love that won't break my heart.

"You know, I can't get used to calling you Jennifer," Catherine pipes in.

"What?" I say, not really listening.

"Your name," she says again. "When I was pregnant I called you something else."

"You named me?"

"I did," she says, "but I guess it's silly."'

I shift on the bench, putting distance between my mother and myself.

"So? What was it?"

"No, no, you'll laugh."

"Come on," I say.

Catherine rolls her shoulders back and sits up taller. "Well, I was a huge fan of *Gone with the Wind*. I read that book like a hundred times and I just loved how strong Scarlet was—unstoppable."

"You were not going to name me Scarlet?" I interrupt.

"No, no," she says, waving me off. "I named you Tara, you know, after that plantation. I just thought it was such a wonderful name but you know, I was just a young girl . . . "

She laughs and shakes her head at herself. "Isn't that silly? My mother always said I had my head in the clouds."

She was going to name me Tara.

I cannot laugh with her and I start to cry.

"What?" she asks. "What did I say?"

THE SUN DROPS below a line of hills and long ribbons of gold and gray light reflect on the high clouds.

We hold hands while I drive Catherine back to the airport.

"What will come next?" she asks.

I am taken aback by her question. It seems foolish in retrospect but all I anticipated and expected was today. What else could there possibly be?

"I don't know," I finally manage to say. "What do you want?"

Catherine tugs on the hem of her silk top and sits taller in her seat. "Well, I want to know you," she says with the authority of a mother. "I want us to be in each other's lives. You could move to Reno. That would solve a lot of our problems."

I pull into the airport parking lot and laugh as if that's a good one. Reno!

She's not laughing.

I turn off the car and tuck the keys into my purse. "Well," I say, clearing my throat. "My life is here, in Portland."

Catherine pouts a little, as if I have burst her bubble, and did she really think I would move to Nevada?

The engine ticks as it cools down and we sit in the quiet for a long time.

The experts who specialize in reunion between first mothers and adopted children suggest a slow and careful "getting to know each other period." Birth parents are warned to be cautious and respectful during reunion. Adoptive children must learn how to believe again. Bridges of trust must be built. Old wounds need to heal.

Of course, I have read all these books. Catherine has read none. I've spent a lifetime in pursuit of healing. Catherine has spent a lifetime in pursuit of hiding. A few days ago, I had been a secret she planned to take to her grave.

With the way I am feeling at this moment—unwanted, rejected, and forgotten—what comes next should be this: Catherine should go away and I should continue with my life. The end.

"We can try to know each other," she says. "Can't we? I would be so sad not to know you."

"You would?" I ask.

She nods and gives the impression of sincerity. "And you have to meet Jessie, she's dying to know you. Daniel too. Oh my goodness, you have such a big family."

I bite the edge of my lip, completely lost. Yes, it would be great to meet Jessie too, but I already knew Daniel isn't in the least interested in me. His wife wrote an email, apologizing for the fact the man hadn't reached out yet. She suggested I be patient.

It had only been a few days and already these people asked a lot of me. Move to Reno? Be patient with the elusive Daniel? Make it a priority to meet Jessie?

A part of me knew I had done all I could do. I had brought Catherine to Portland. I booked and paid for her flight. I gave her this day and my time.

But another part of me, that tiny part so hungry for family and a mother, took over and I nodded yes.

I agree to know her, to know them. I agree to try.

She lights up, as if delighted. She laughs out loud. The sound fills the inside of my car and makes me think of Jo. My mother and my daughter have the same laugh.

WE GET OUT of the car and walk in silence, holding hands once again. As we approach the airport terminal, I feel shaky and scared. What have I agreed to?

"Saying goodbye is supposed to be the hardest part," I hear myself say, quoting one of my adoption books. "If we are going to be in each other's lives, you need to call me, in a few days. We're also supposed to make a plan to see each other again. We are supposed to set a definite date."

Catherine and I separate and go down the escalator. When we reach the bottom, she doesn't try to hold my hand again. In the passage from the top of the stairs to the bottom, she has become someone in a hurry to get home.

She walks ahead of me, eyes trained on the glowing blue screen

that displays the schedule for the departing flights. "Well, I can definitely call you although I'm not sure when," Catherine says over her
shoulder. "And I'm not sure when we can get together again either. I
have a lot of things coming up, things I've already scheduled months
in advance—"

Catherine strides over to the security checkpoint and digs into
her purse for her ticket.

Dragging behind her, my hands get cold, and I open and close
them to bring back circulation.

"Okay, well, I guess I don't need to know exactly when we can
meet again," I begin but she doesn't seem to be listening as she gath-
ers up her license and her boarding pass.

I feel waves of fear that cannot be rationalized. *She's leaving.
She's leaving me again.*

When we get to the front of the line, Catherine puts her arm
around my shoulder. She gives me a quick hug and a kiss on the
cheek. It's a peck, like we are strangers.

"Okay," she says. "So I'll call you when I get home. I'll try to
call tonight."

"Okay," I say. "But I feel like we might need to know, tentatively,
when to meet again. Do you have *any* idea when you might be free?"

It's like asking a disinterested guy for a date. I'm setting myself
up to be rejected and here it comes.

She does this little shift from one foot to the other. She is restless. She sighs. "Well, not really," she says. "Why don't I figure that
out when I get home."

I tell myself that her reassurance should be enough. I want to believe we will form a plan later but my body tells a different truth. Catherine left me before and she will leave me again and she is leaving me right now. If she truly meant to know me and be in my life, she would not behave this way. She would stand still. She would look me in the eye.

I hug myself and try, one more time.

"Are you sure?" I ask. "Will you figure it out? Will you remember?"

"Yes, yes, I will, I promise," she says. She hugs me once again but it's an impatient embrace. She is eager to get on her way.

I step off to the side and let my mother go on without me.

Catherine weaves though the maze of security, shoulders back and hips slung forward. When she reaches the x-ray machines, she slips out of her high-heel sandals.

My face is wet but I don't wipe away the evidence of tears. I let myself cry and hug myself tighter still. Is this the fear, terror, grief, and rage that I felt as a baby? The pain makes me dizzy. How did I survive?

Catherine forgot to ask: *How are you here, Jennifer? How did you make it without me?*

She also forgot to say she was so sorry for leaving me. That she would do anything to make it up to me—her first child—her daughter.

She rushes back to a full life of children, grandchildren—her big extended family. I watch from here—as unknown to her as I was when she arrived this morning.

Catherine exits the x-ray machine and bends over to push her feet into her strappy sandals. In a final gesture, as if it is enough, she lifts her arm and waves goodbye.

TWENTY-FIVE

REUNION

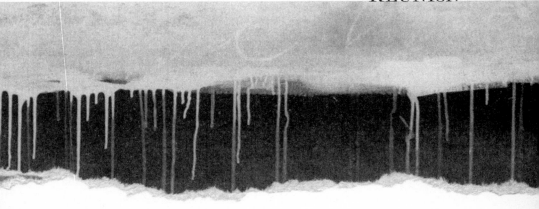

WHEN I RETURN TO THE HOUSE, I pull into the driveway and Spencer and Jo explode from the front door.

Cries of "Moooom!" pierce through the closed windows of the car.

I am shaky and unsteady, my eyes are puffy from tears spent at the airport, but now it's going to be okay. I shove the keys into my purse and get out of the car. The kids bound down the stairs, elbows and long legs and pure hearts. They throw themselves against my body.

I want them to. I need them to.

"Mooooooom!" Jo yells, pressing her face into my stomach.

"We missed you, Mom," Spencer yells, hugging around my shoulders.

They feel so good and I'm so lucky for their love.

"How did it go?" Spencer asks. "Was she nice? Are you going to see her again?"

"Mom, Mom, Mom," Jo says. She doesn't ask about Catherine.

Roger is on the porch, watching the scene and has a big grin of welcome on his face too. He waves and I lift my hand.

"Come on," I say, wiping at my eyes. "Let's go in. I'll tell you everything."

Jo tugs my arm, the signal she wants to be lifted and I scoop her up to my hip. She wraps her arms around my neck and presses her face into my shoulder. It's like she wants to crawl into my skin and the funny thing is—I finally get this desire now. Didn't I want to crawl into Catherine's skin? Don't I still?

With Jo on one side, I put my arm around Spencer's shoulders and we all go up the steps together—this six-legged crowd of awkwardness. "Was she nice?" Spencer asks again.

"She was super nice," I say.

"Will you see her again?" he asks. "Will we meet her?"

"I don't know, Honey," I say. "I just need to think about everything. We'll see."

At the top of the steps, I kiss Roger hello over the top of Jo's head.

"We made a party for you, Mom!" Jo announces, wiggling down from my side.

"A tea party," Roger adds.

I nod like a tea party is just great.

I don't need to tell Roger how I feel or what's going on with Catherine. He already knows since I called from the airport and told him about the day.

"Come on, come see," Jo says. She races around Roger, wanting to be the first one in the house and to show off what they've been cooking up, which I already know—since Jo is a tea party expert—will be a dozen tiny plates of snack foods, big pots of fresh mint tea, and candles flickering in tiny cups.

Roger goes into the house too but before I can move, Spencer stops me at the threshold. He turns me to face him, his hands on my shoulders and it's funny the way he does this.

"Let me look at you," he says.

Spencer peers into my face—into my eyes.

"You're different," he says.

I don't really get it yet—this biological surge of sensory information that has passed from Catherine to me in our one afternoon together—but Spencer does. He looks at a person he's been looking at his entire life and there is a confidence in his voice.

"You're better," he adds.

CATHERINE DOES CALL, the next morning after our meeting, and she continues to call. She tries to stay connected over the next few days. She does her best.

But she's not coming to see me again. She makes this clear on the phone. "I don't like to travel. I have things to do. I'm busy, you know."

These are normal things that normal people say. I understand and a part of me, that stranger part of me who realizes we do not know each other, cuts my mother an ocean of slack. But the other part of me is a blender of complex emotional response. I need her, I ache for her, I want her, and I am so pissed off too. I'm sad, scared, confused, worried, and a million other shades of feeling.

This duality—established at our first conversation—becomes the defining quality of our reunion. I am full of need and I am full of understanding.

Catherine doesn't admit need from her end of our reunion. She has the same feelings and desires that I do, I know she does, but her life has been largely lived and not largely explored. She likes things to be nice and easy. She likes to have fun. She doesn't seek understanding. She believes she understands well enough.

I would say that Catherine thinks of me like a new girlfriend, an acquaintance that she is trying to incorporate into her life. In this way, she can keep me at a distance while trying to be polite. But the truth is, she is also pissed because I'm not a new girlfriend. I am an old secret and the way she had it worked out, I was supposed to stay hidden. She has to be furious with her new pal. Of course, I'm just guessing.

THE ADOPTION BOOKS are accurate when they report that an adoptee *needs* to be close to the birth mother and to have some form of regular contact. After ten days pass without a plan to meet, I feel I am going insane. I have to take some action for myself and my own well-being.

I make a call.

"I've booked a flight. I'm coming at the end of the week, just for a couple days," I blurt over the telephone line.

"Oh," Catherine says. "Well, that's kind of short notice."

It sounds like she is at work. Her voice has a professional clip.

"I'll stay in a hotel . . . " I stammer. My stomach churns. "I won't impose. We can just visit when you have time."

"It's only been ten days, crimeinee," she says. Her voice is like a knife.

I almost say that I won't come.

I almost hang up the phone.

"It's fine. It's fine," she concedes, just in time. "Just come. Jessie can't wait to meet you anyway."

SUNDAY MORNING, 7:00 AM, I am booked on the earliest flight to Reno. Standing in line to get on the plane, I'm on the phone with Jessie and she's totally pissed. Fire feels like it is coming out of the phone. "Fine, you don't want me at the airport, I get it," she says.

"It's not that I don't want to meet you," I say. "I need to just do this one person at a time, Catherine first, then more people can come in but this is really intense. I don't think I can handle more people, right away."

Jessie says nothing more but I feel her on the other side of the line, tapping her foot and drumming her fingers on her kitchen countertop.

"It's fine," Jessie finally says again.

"It's not personal, Jessie," I say, "please understand."

"I do, I do, I totally understand," she says, only her voice is not understanding.

"Jessie, come on, I'll see you when I get there," I say. "I cannot wait."

I hand my ticket to the man at the gate and he scans the numbers with a computerized wand. Converging with the rest of the passengers, I go down the long walkway that funnels travelers into the belly of the plane.

"Come over after I have a couple hours with Catherine, please?"

"Well, I don't know. I've got a lot to do today," Jessie says. "Anyway, I gotta go."

She hangs up the telephone, gone as fast a hummingbird.

All that has happened is that I've asked to see Catherine first, just for a couple of hours, and then I will meet Jessie in the afternoon. This is the way it needs to be—the child who was given away needs to have some control as she returns to the world of those who rejected her, but Jessie is not interested in psychology.

What gets me is not that she's pissed. What gets me is that she is pissed in the same way I get pissed. She is abrupt, hurt, and incredibly fast to react and then she is off protecting herself with excuses of being busy.

I've behaved in exactly the same way for most of my life and now I get to see that this is the way my people are. I thought I was so wounded before—incapable of managing slights and hurts and disappointments. No, that wasn't it. This is how my people deal with pain. They get snippy, they hang up the phone, they run away.

"Welcome to Southwest," a flight attendant says.

I hear myself say thanks and walk down the aisle, smiling this weird, stupid smile. I should be really upset with this situation with my sister but I'm not. I'm learning about myself by the simple act of engaging with her.

"Please fasten your seat belt," comes the voice of a flight attendant, from the front of the plane. "And turn off all electronic devices."

I buckle myself in and take a deep breath. Here we go.

TWENTY-SIX

BREAKFAST IN RENO

RENO AIR IS like no other—it is bright and crisp and laced with the smell of sage. Reno air is mountain air with a bite.

When I step off the plane in Reno, the old smell hits me.

The next blow is that my mother isn't waiting.

Slot machines, cigarette smoke, and strangers greet me instead.

Welcome home.

I weave down the long corridor that leads through the terminal, passing signs advertising all manner of entertainment from hookers to musicals. If I believed the postings on the walls, I'd be at a casino as fast as a Checker Cab could get me there and I'd be feeding my silver dollars into a Wheel of Fortune machine.

Janet used to say, "You cannot win playing another man's game," and this was how she felt about gambling. Did I make that up? Was the voice of reason born inside of me, all on my own? I cannot say with one hundred percent certainty but I do not gamble with my money. I only take risks with my heart.

CATHERINE HAS LEFT a message on my phone and says she will meet me at the curb, since parking is such a hassle.

If this were Denver, Chicago, or New York City, I'd get the whole excuse about parking hassles and the need to keep things simple. But Reno International is only large in name. At this time in the morning, on a Sunday, the Reno airport is like a ghost town. A dried wheel of sagebrush actually rolls past, pushed by the morning wind as I snap my phone closed.

Yes, Catherine is pissed.

No, she really didn't want me to come.

Yes, my heart is broken.

No, I'm not surprised.

I cry as I stand at the curb, waiting.

I wonder if this is too much for me to bear? I ask myself if I need to just toss in the towel and go home now?

I ask myself the question of all questions—the one I always ask when I can't take care of myself: *What if it was Josephine instead of you?*

The answer is so clear when put into that context, and I am about to turn around and go back to buy a return flight when a huge blazer roars up to the curb.

Catherine drives the rig like she's a cowgirl on a horse and waves her hand, only the gesture is impatient, as if I am a task on a to-do list that she doesn't want to be responsible for.

Catherine pulls on the emergency break and gets out of her rig. She comes around to give me a quick hug and I'm there, in my pathetic sadness—crying and lost. I'm a forty-four-year-old baby. What could be worse?

Something about my tears makes her even more impatient and she sighs.

She hugs me, just for a second, and then tries to let go but I won't let her get away. I hold on to her familiar body, close my eyes, and breathe in her smell. I can't help myself. I just have to do this. She is my mother, my very own mother. How can I not hug this woman? How can I not want her?

"I missed you," I hear myself say.

She pats at my back, exasperated, impatient, and distracted. But does she also soften? Is there something that gives way in her? I want to believe it's true. I want to believe she wants me too.

"Okay, it's okay," she says, clearing her throat. "Let's get you into the truck."

THE DRIVE TO her place is filled with chatter. She talks about how upset Jessie is, as if I didn't know, and apparently there is some problem at work as well. It's important, what she is saying, these details of her immediate life, but I don't follow her line of thinking or reasoning. It hurts to think in that way—to take in intellectual information. While she talks, I nod and smile as if I am following along but what really goes on is that I am taking in—as deeply as I can—the timbre of her voice. It's so musical and right. And look at her! My hungry eyes reconfirm that she looks just right with those long fingers, long legs, and her slim womanly body.

Like I did in Portland, I absorb her into my senses, only this time, being with her is that much more precious. I know this moment will not last. I know I may never see her again. I know I have to make the most of our time together.

Finally she runs out of talk and reaches over to touch my arm.

"I'm so glad you're here," Catherine says. "It was a hassle, rearranging everything, but now I see you, I am really glad."

"I'm sorry it was a hassle," I say.

"Oh, pooh," she says, waving me off.

SHE MAKES A few turns and we are in a neighborhood of tract houses—cookie cutter lookalikes. The colors are indistinct whites and tans.

"Home sweet home," she says, pushing a button to open the garage.

I won't stay here with her; rather, I have a hotel, but we have agreed to start here. Jessie will come soon and then we'll have breakfast.

Catherine leads the way and her garage is tidy. She has a few pieces of painted furniture, which resemble the furniture in Jo's room.

In through the back door, past the laundry room, down a narrow hall, and we're in an open area that is the living room, dining room, and kitchen. Trotting over to meet Catherine is a huge black cat. Another cat sits in the middle of the living room and it is a skeleton covered with hair.

"There's my babies," Catherine says. She talks baby talk and scoops up the smaller cat with its fur mottled the colors of beige, orange, gray, black, and white. The animal hangs as limp as dirty laundry. "This is Sadie," Catherine explains, "she's got cancer."

I keep my hands behind my back—being allergic and all. "I'm sorry," I say.

"I just love her so-oooo much," Catherine says, nuzzling into the furry bones and poor Sadie has the face of a Muppet. That cat is very close to death.

Catherine lets Sadie drip to the floor and heaves the big black one into her arms.

"This is Shadow. He's the one with diabetes. I have to give him a shot twice a day, which is why it's so hard for me to travel."

Catherine rolls the cat in her arms until his white belly is up and he bats around at her face.

The phone rings and Catherine rolls the big cat under her arm like he's a sack of flour.

"That's going to be Jessie," she warns and her voice holds the question, *Can she come?* Already I pick up on the nuance and I've known her for less than a month.

"It's fine."

Catherine snaps open the phone and before even saying hi, she says, "Come over. It's okay."

While they chat, I wander around the living room. Her home feels like she feels. Tidy, contained, beautiful.

She has all-white furniture and white wall-to-wall carpeting. A crucifix hangs on the wall, there are vanilla-scented pillar candles, and a glass coffee table.

There is no garden in her yard; it's just grass and big decorative stones. At the edge of her yard is a tall fence connecting her to all her neighbors.

"Well, dry your hair and come on over, honestly," Catherine says into the phone, snapping with impatience. While I don't care for her tone, it helps to hear her be pissed at someone else. I don't take it so personally—or at least the earlier demonstrations of impatience don't cut so deep.

Catherine flips her phone closed.

"She'll be a few minutes, maybe twenty. Should I make coffee?"

"Coffee is good," I say.

Catherine tosses Shadow down and the cat ambles a few steps before rolling on its side like a water balloon. It bats at the air with its black paws.

Catherine goes into her kitchen, talking about how she loves her little coffee machine, since it makes one cup at a time.

I drift down the hall, nodding like I'm listening, but I'm not.

She has a lot of flowers in her home, mostly made of silk. On the wall there are hanging plates painted with the faces of movie stars from the '50s—Yul Brynner in *The King and I*, Clark Gable hunched over Vivien Leigh in *Gone with the Wind*. Down the hall and around the corner is her guest bath, all white with a white linen shower curtain. On the white counter, on a small plate, are pretty pastel shell-shaped soaps—which I know Jo would love.

In fact, what I think as I move through Catherine's house is how she is so much like Jo. Feminine and delicate. There is a level of innocence here too.

Out of the bathroom and into the guest room, I stop at a row of photos and there is Jo looking up at me from a black-and-white photo of a little girl in a tutu, tights, and ballet shoes. But that's not Jo. That's my mother when she was little. I look at the black-and-white for a long time.

Was my mother well loved as a little girl?

From the looks of the photo—smiling child in a tutu—I would say yes.

I would also say she has been very lucky.

I WEAVE DOWN the hall and past her bedroom, which I do not go into. I feel like that is too personal a threshold. That is her private world but of course, I make note of all those pillows and the cozy bed. I have the same set up at home.

One more room is her office and I wander in, keeping my arms crossed over myself.

Catherine has a PC computer on a tidy desk and little-kid art is taped to the walls—modest little rainbows and stick figures holding hands. The message "We love you Grammy" is written in the hand of a child.

The art is subdued compared to Jo's—she creates her work as if she were Chagall. Jo's rainbows and princesses are a riot of color. She uses all of the white space on her paper too.

The fat cat, Shadow, positions himself in the door of the office.

His chin is up and his eyes are slats regarding me as if to say, "Who the hell are you?"

I make my hand into a claw and hiss but the creature doesn't even blink.

WHILE I STUDY a wall of framed photos, Catherine finally arrives with a flowered mug.

"I hope it's okay, my looking around," I say.

She waves her hand in that way, like brushing me off, and I guess this means that she doesn't care at all. She gets the big cat in her arms again, cradling him like a baby and rocks from side to side.

"I want you to be comfortable in my house," she says. "It's fine."

She has changed in the time I have been here. She is less angry and impatient. The edge has slipped away. She seems fragile and young.

I hold the mug she has offered, warming my hands, and I take a careful sip.

"This is great," I say, "what did you put into it?"

"Just Coffee-mate creamer," she laughs, "and coffee."

"It's good."

"I worried I added too much cream."

"No, it's perfect," I say. And it's true. It's really good and I don't even like coffee.

We stand together, a little awkward and unsure.

"Your house is very pretty," I say.

"Thanks," she says, looking around like seeing her world for the first time.

There is a clatter at the front of the house and Catherine jumps a little with surprise.

"Mom?" comes a voice.

"There's Jessie," Catherine says, dropping the cat on the floor.

She leaves me in the office and I hear their voices mix in the living room. They speak in hushed whispers.

Like a coward, I hide in the office. How will I handle a sibling? What is the protocol?

I look to Shadow, as if he can give some clue, but the cat is useless. He just folds over on his side and whacks at the air again.

Taking a deep breath, pulling on my stores of courage, I step over Shadow and walk up the hall.

BASED ON HER voice, I expected a pert, tiny woman with wide hips and a tight jaw but Jessie is something altogether different. She is Catherine with more dramatic coloring—dark hair and brows.

"Look at you," I say, "my goodness you are so tall."

"Me! Look at you," Jessie says, grinning. She is just adorable. Her smile lights up her whole face.

As I put the mug on the counter, we share a quick, awkward embrace.

"Oh my god," Jessie says, "she has my forehead and my chin."

"And your hair," Catherine says. "Feel her hair."

Jessie touches my hair and I do the same, which feels like my own.

"She definitely has your jaw," Jessie says, "and Daniel's eyes."

"She's got Bill's nose," Catherine adds.

They talk about me as if I'm not there and you'd think it would be offensive. You'd think I'd want to distinguish myself and say I'm uniquely myself but I don't want that, nor do I feel that. There is comfort in how I look like them in hair and eyes and chin, part of a clan—familiar—family.

A hush falls over us and it's like wind whistling over a lonely salt flat. An immeasurable feeling sweeps through me. I can tell in the quiet of my mother and sister that they are thinking, but what? What are they thinking?

"Let's eat," Catherine says.

"Good idea," comes my instant agreement and we bundle out of the house and back into the big truck.

THE PLACE THEY choose for our first meal together is across from a mini mall. It's like a retro burger joint—oversized laminated menus, red vinyl booths, and a white-and-black checkered floor.

Jessie makes a point to position me next to Catherine on one side of the booth, a move that feels weird since I think they are used to sitting next to each other. Jessie sits across from us, elbows on the table, and she grins as she looks from her mother to me and back to her mother again.

A waitress brings us huge, red, plastic tumblers of ice water and we order from the breakfast menu—bacon, pancakes, hash browns.

After she goes, they chat a little about their own lives and there is a comfort between them. They make easy jokes with each other and the relationship seems more like sisters than mother and daughter.

I just sit back and become observer of this life they've made without me, as if I never was.

Jessie pats the table with her hand and swings her attention to me again.

"When you first called," Jessie says, "I went on the Internet and read everything ever written about you."

"That's right, she did," Catherine agrees.

"I saw this article about how you baked your own muffins with fresh berries that you picked on some hiking trek. I called mom to say, 'She's like a hippie Martha Stewart.' I would never do something like that."

"That's right," Catherine agrees. "She sent me every one of those damn articles, like I have time to read them."

"You should read them, geez."

"I don't have time to read all that crap; Daniel's working me to death."

"Tell him to knock it off."

"Right, tell Daniel to knock it off."

"I'm telling you, tell him to knock it off—want me to call?"

"No, I don't want you to call, I can handle Daniel myself."

"Oh, like you are handling him now," Jessie says.

Jessie lifts one dark eyebrow high on her forehead and looks at me like I might agree with the point she's making, only I'm over here, clueless.

Hippie Martha Stewart?

I'm not a fucking hippie, I want to say. What the hell does that mean? Only, I guess to a Reno girl, I am a fucking hippie. I just sit there, a Ping-Pong ball that goes from being offended to being entertained. Irritated and then forgiving, I'm short-circuited and unable to process what's been said.

And then there's this story about the MIA brother Daniel and all I know is that Catherine works for him, at his cabinet company, and that they do not get along.

Should I jump into the family drama?

If I do, won't that backfire on me?

And what do I know about it anyway?

Again, I am without words.

Thankfully, I don't have to decide because the food comes and I am able to disappear into a stack of pancakes.

TWENTY-SEVEN

JACKPOT

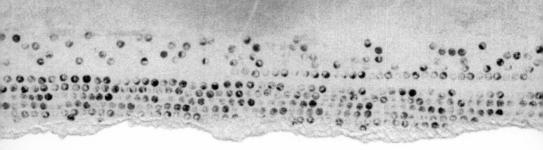

AFTER MY MORNING with Catherine and then Jessie, I'm so worn down, I go to bed and sleep through to the next morning.

Of course, this response makes sense. Look at babies. They are with us for a while and then they sleep as if they were dead.

Since meeting Catherine, I sleep a deep exhausted sleep that feels like death. I don't even dream and when I wake up, my whole body is heavy.

WHEN I FINALLY drag myself from bed, I draw a bath and float in the hottest water I can stand.

The telephone rings and I shake the water off my hand as I pick up the phone.

"Good morning," I say.

"It's not morning," Catherine says.

"Good afternoon?"

"What are you doing?" she asks.

"I'm in the tub," I say. "Just hanging out."

"Well, get out of the tub, get into some clothes," she says. "We're going to have lunch."

"We are?"

"Actually," she says, "Daniel is coming too, he just doesn't know it yet."

I sit up, bubbles skimming down my chest.

"What?"

"Don't worry, I've got this covered," Catherine says, "half an hour."

She hangs up and I lean back in the tub again.

Catherine is like a steamroller but then again, aren't I exactly the same?

She's so bossy and confident and annoying.

Aren't I all those things?

I have to laugh at this new view of myself, which is not an entirely pleasant view. Taking a deep breath, I get myself into action. Half an hour isn't much time.

IT'S A WORKDAY, Monday, and Catherine is dressed up for being in the office. She wears a silk blouse and slim-fitting pants in a pretty color of green. When she sees me in the lobby, she rushes over.

"There you are," she says, taking hold of my arm. "I was worried. What took you so long? Are you okay?"

She can already tell what's going on inside of me—like a mother—and it's unnerving. I feel like I am going to cry from being so nervous and scared. From what I've overheard, Daniel sounds like a very mean person. I don't think I can handle mean today.

"I'm just nervous," I say. "Is he here?"

"Yes, he's already sitting down. I'm sorry," Catherine says, "I know I sprung this on you at the last minute but I just want to get this over with. Just meet him and then that will be done."

She leads the way through the packed restaurant, a place called Chili's, which is supposed to be a favorite of Daniel's.

She holds my hand and walks with great, long, confident strides— pulling me along. I shake so hard, I feel like I will throw up.

She turns a corner and leads us down a long row of tables. Pretty soon, we are in front of a huge, red, plastic booth and there he is, the man I've seen in all the photos. Daniel.

When he looks up from his menu, his expression is not that of a stranger. He seems truly amazed to behold me.

"You're Jennifer?" he asks.

I nod like yes, of course.

He laughs and in that sound, I'd swear I've known him my entire life even though we look at each other for the first time.

Catherine stands back and laughs too, for her own reasons. "I told you," she says. "I told you."

Daniel tries to stand up, thighs hitting the table and it's a little awkward to reach each other. After a scoot and push, finally he comes around the table and we hug each other. Daniel feels just great and what a skyscraper of a man. A brother. I've had a brother all this time.

Just what is the mystery contained in DNA? What is the energetic wavelength that moves within family units? What don't we
know, despite all our scientific strides and advances? As I hug my
brother and see my own mysterious knowing fall into place, I can
only say that I knew of his existence—I did.

Daniel ushers his wife out of the booth and says she is Rona. I
offer my hand but then that seems weird and instead we hug too.

Why not? We're one big happy family now, right?

Rona is a small woman with deep-set eyes and a pretty face.
She says, "You sweet thing, you're shaking like a leaf." She holds my
hands and seems very sincere.

WE ALL SETTLE into the booth again, the three of them on one side
with Daniel in the middle and me on the other side. Alone.

Water arrives in giant, red, plastic tumblers as if they are standard issue here in the Biggest Little City in the World.

I stare over my megasized cup and study this brother.

Daniel, doing the same, puts his elbows on the table and holds
his hands together, just like Jessie did yesterday at breakfast. I sit
back and hold my own hands in my lap.

Somehow, like a miracle, food gets ordered and Catherine claps
her hands like calling this meeting to order.

"Well, here we are," Catherine says and she laughs as if she has
told a joke.

Daniel laughs with her and then rolls his eyes like she's on his
last nerve. Rona laughs in the same way, coughing into her fist.

"When Catherine said we were all meeting for lunch . . . " Rona begins, from the far side of Daniel.

" . . . Well, I told her forget it. No way. I have a million things to do today," Daniel says. He makes big gestures, like I do, like Catherine does, using his hands while he talks.

"Which isn't to say he didn't want to meet you . . . " Rona explains.

" . . . No," Daniel says, "of course not."

"Daniel just has so much going on and Catherine caught us by surprise . . . " Rona says.

The two women smile at each other and Catherine does a quick shrug like everyone just needs to get over it. " . . . I just wanted you to meet my daughter. After all, she's here," Catherine says, finishing the sentence.

"She has a way of catching us all by surprise," Daniel says, with another eye roll.

More laughter all around.

I'm nodding like I understand and it all makes sense but really, I'm just stalling because I don't know what to say. It's like the breakfast with Jessie. I'm too amazed to speak more than a grunt and a few simple words.

When the laughter dies down, Daniel becomes serious.

"Mom says you're a Buddhist, is that right?"

"Well, um," I begin. I glance at Catherine and she grins and nods like I should go ahead and confess. "Something like that."

Daniel is like a laser beam of focus, all business now, and I'd hate to negotiate with him. I bet he's tough!

"So what's the bottom line here? Do Buddhists believe in God?"

I take a quick look at Rona, who seems equally interested and then I can only look at my own hands.

"Well, um," I hear myself say again. "I suppose."

"Oh, Daniel," Catherine says, slapping at his arm, "leave her alone."

After that, we downshift to politics and since it happens to be an election year (McCain versus Obama), they collectively talk about the possibility of "that man" making it into office. "That man" being Obama. Catherine talks about her admiration of Sarah Palin and how she hopes this country has the good sense to put such a bright lady in office.

I can only shrug and say I'm not really political.

Finally, we make an even deeper downshift and find the mutual ground of children. Daniel and Rona tell me about their daughter. I talk about Spencer and Josephine.

"I'm just dying to meet them," Daniel says.

"Daniel just loves kids," Rona adds.

"He's wonderful with them too," Catherine adds.

PRETTY SOON, SALADS are eaten and the water is gone and Daniel, Rona, and Catherine are like a team of stockbrokers before the exchange opens. They check their watches, read their text messages, and tap at their phones. Time to get back to work.

As we leave the restaurant, Rona and Catherine pull together a loose plan for all of us to meet for pizza tonight. Rona wants me to meet her daughter, Brittney, and Catherine wants Jessie to bring her kids over too.

I sway a little, imagining another layer of family and my stomach rolls with nausea. All I want to do is sleep again but I nod like yes, pizza would great.

Daniel is strangely quiet and when he hugs me, I can tell emotion rises in him—some old sadness that I don't know but that I certainly recognize. I want to ask him what's going on but he lifts a hand between us like I need to give him room. He has tears in his eyes.

Later, Rona will tell me that this was happiness. Daniel was just so happy to meet me.

AFTER THEY LEAVE, it's just Catherine and me again. We stand close to each other, in the parking lot, next to her car. Our bodies—so much the same—do not touch.

"That went great, didn't it?" she says. "I think that went really great."

Her blue-gray eyes look tired, as if this meeting took a huge effort.

"It did," I say. "You did a good job."

"Me?" she says. "You did a great job. I'm so glad you're here. I'm so glad you're my daughter."

She touches my cheek, the lightest glance of a touch and in that moment, I am so thankful I had the guts to come to Reno and to endure meeting all these people.

In a Reno parking lot, I am someone's daughter and I get to

feel how it is to have my mother be happy to have me around. It's the best gift. Better than gold, and no, I have not made a bad gamble with my heart.

TWENTY-EIGHT

Just Three Again

"Does it feel real?" Jo asks.

"What, Honey?" I ask.

"Finding your mother?"

We are in Jo's bed, waking up to a new day. No school. Cartoons and cinnamon rolls on the horizon. The drapes that surround Jo's canopy bed are pulled closed—making a fortress she calls "the girls only zone."

"I suppose it does," I say. "Why do you ask?"

"Well," she says. "I know it's happened but it doesn't feel real. It's more like a dream."

I study her heart-shaped face, her dove-gray eyes, and her curling blond hair that comes to her chin.

"Maybe because we are here, together?" I ask. "And she is somewhere else? Is that what you mean?"

"I guess, but it's more than that," Jo says. "It's like you've always been here and she has never been here."

I curl my knees under her bottom and have my arm under her neck. Our fingers are intertwined the way she likes. She calls it "cuddle time."

"I guess you're right," I say. "It is like a dream."

It's been two months since I met Catherine and I'm keeping my kids separate from the reunion because it's hard to figure out a way to mesh our two worlds—and our two ways of being. In Reno, Catherine is a delight, but when I come home, she is not.

She is not willing to come to Portland. She is also not willing to call on a regular basis. And she will not help me pick a date to come see her.

To make it worse, Daniel had made plans to come to Portland and then—at the last minute—cancelled. He was busy with work. He did not reschedule.

Spencer had been so excited to meet his new uncle—excitement that had been built within him by my own overblown enthusiasm.

It was one thing to be sketchy with me—to yank me around—but my kids did not deserve that kind of treatment. For my own, I could be protective.

Unlike Spencer and me, who keep our hearts out for all to see, Jo wasn't upset about Daniel—not in the least. She keeps herself far away from all the drama—maybe that's just her way. She likes to stay quiet and think about things. I appreciate that quality.

"Do you think you might want to meet her, Honey?" I ask. "Someday?"

Jo purses her lips together, as if kissing the air. "I don't know."

Before I can ask another question, Spencer pushes the drapes open and says, "Hey!"

Jo jumps up and takes a defensive posture—hands on her hips with her long fingers splayed wide.

"Girls ONLY!" she yells. "Go away."

"Ha!" Spencer says. "I can be here if I want. Right, Mom?"

"Yes, yes, come on. Scoot over, Jo, make room."

Jo throws herself back on the bed and we all readjust to fit three.

"You were talking about your mom, weren't you?"

"A little," I say.

Spencer nods but says nothing. He smells like morning breath and boy. He's going into puberty. Soon there will be underarm deodorant in the medicine chest for him.

"Are you glad you looked for her?" he asks.

They both look at me, waiting for the answer.

"Yes," I say. "I am so glad."

"Would you do it again," he asks, "if you had to it over?"

"Yes," I say.

It's quiet again and I wonder what's coming next. Will he ask when he will meet her or if I'm still mad and hurt about the Daniel thing?

"Do you think it's over with her?" Spencer asks.

"Over?"

"Do you think you'll ever see her again?"

"Oh, sure," I say. "Maybe, well. I don't know . . . "

I stop because I don't know what else to say. I take a deep breath and back the story up, in order to give the widest view. I try to explain to them how it was for my mother to be a young girl in 1963, giving up a baby and having her heart broken. I talk about living a lifetime with such a big secret and how it is hard for her—and for me—to figure out a way to be together.

I try to speak slowly and with care.

"Maybe Catherine and I can't be together now—or for a while," I say. "I don't know. But I'm glad I found her and I know she's glad too."

It's like story time and I have to stop the book midway.

"I just don't now what's going to happen in the end, you guys," I say. "We'll have to wait and see."

Jo pops up and grins. "Well I know how it ends," she says.

"You do?" I say.

"Sure!" she says and she nods over at Spencer who must understand because he sits up too.

"You have us," Spencer says.

"Right," says Jo. "You live happily ever after with Princess Josephine and Lord Spencer. The End!"

Spencer nods in total agreement.

They both seem very pleased with themselves and even though I am supposed to be the writer, I couldn't have created a better end myself.

TWENTY-NINE

FORGIVING

THE LEAVES OF THE RED OAK TREE finally fall from the tree. They float on the breeze and cover the green lawn to make a mosaic of decay.

It is nearly Halloween.

A knock comes at the back door, knuckles against glass. Spencer and Jo race up the basement steps, a clatter of bodies. "Daaaaaad!" the kids yell.

Spencer pulls the back door open and together they tackle Steve where he waits on the back porch. Their love is like the love of Labrador pups—unbounded.

"Hey, you guys ready?" he asks, laughing and patting their backs.

"We want to finish," Spencer starts.

"Yeah, we're watching *Cyberchase*," Jo finishes.

"It's a double header," Spencer adds.

"Well, *Cyberchase!*" Steve winks over at me. "You can't miss that."

"Just five more minutes," Spencer says.

"Well, okay," Steve says.

"Come in," I say. "You want coffee?"

"Um sure, if it's no trouble."

The kids tumble down the steps again and the TV blares. I pour Steve a cup of coffee and he lingers at the back door, as if ready to make a quick getaway. He says something about fall and how he can't believe it's here so soon. "So many leaves to rake," he says.

I nod.

After four years apart, we have come to an uneasy peace. Divorce is awkward. You make plans, you have dreams, you fail, you fall, you get up, and you start again. I know we're okay. He's dating. Roger is in my life. It's going to be fine.

"You know, you're really different," Steve says—breaking into my thoughts.

"Ha ha," I say. I think he's about to crack a joke.

"No, I mean it. You're more, I don't know, grounded or something."

I lean against the edge of the counter and cross my arms over my stomach, a habit I've gotten into these days. I squint at Steve, trying to see if he is saying what I think he is saying. Is he really that perceptive?

"Well, you know I found my first mother?" I venture.

"Yeah, Spencer told me," he says. "I was going to ask but I didn't want to pry."

"I appreciate that," I say.

Steve looks into the mug, as if searching for wisdom in my morning brew.

"Do you want to see a photo?"

He perks up as if this is exactly what he wants and I wave him into the dining room. On the table is the mess of breakfast dishes, Jo Jo's morning creations of butterflies and rainbows drawn with colored pen, Spencer's pile of comic books, and my computer. I bend over the keyboard and bring Catherine's image to the screen. Catherine is there with her gray-blue eyes, auburn hair, and great big fashion-model smile.

I step back and hug myself again.

"Wo-ow."

Steve puts his hand on the table and leans in for a better look.

"She's a knockout. God, she looks just like Jo."

I swell with pride as if I had something to do with Catherine's looks. "And her name is Catherine," I add.

"Like Jo's middle name!"

"And she was going to name me—get this—Tara."

Steve stands back and blinks on this information.

"You are kidding me," he finally says.

"I know," I say, with another swell of pride.

"Did you tell that woman—that teacher?"

"Tylanni?"

"Yeah," he says.

"Yes. She was blown away. Speechless."

Steve can only nod, equally silenced.

"And there's more. When she was in high school and pregnant with me, her tutor's name was—get this—Carmel!"

Steve is now unable to even nod. His mouth hangs open.

"It's like you knew," he finally says.

"I know," I say again. I beam with pride. I did know. I did.

I go on to tell Steve the good parts about how I met Catherine—how she came to Portland and we spent a day together. I describe the way she moves, the sound of her voice, her gestures, her mannerisms, her inflections. I tell him how much alike we are.

As I go on and on, I click through more photos and in the midst of my slideshow, Steve steps back and pushes at the bridge of his nose.

"What?" I ask. "What's wrong?"

He shakes his head, unable to speak.

I am so surprised by the tears that fill his eyes, I rush off to get a paper towel from the kitchen—just to have something to do. I've seen him cry only once, when Spencer was born. Actually twice. He cried when I left. But overall, Steve is a rock.

Back in the dining room, I push the paper towel into his hand.

"She's what you've been looking for all this time," he manages to say.

I touch his arm and then drop my hand. I just stand there, mystified and helpless.

While he grips the paper towel, his face gets red and he clenches his jaw.

What passes through his mind? Is he replaying all the years of our marriage—all the ridiculous fights? Is he seeing our bitter end and the harm we've done to each other?

I am.

"I'm sorry I hurt you, Steve," I say. "If I knew what I had been missing, if there was any way I could have known sooner—"

He shakes off my apology and tosses his hands high as if talking to the ceiling and not to me. "Why didn't I think of it?" he yells.

Throwing the paper towel on the table, he pushes the tears away with the back of his fist. "It's so damn obvious, now that I see her and now I see you with her. God. What an idiot I have been."

He hits his forehead and I grab his arm to stop the blow. "No. It's not your fault. It was me. I expected too much from you, from the marriage. You couldn't be my whole family. You couldn't fill in for all that loss."

I don't even know what I am saying. I just can't bear Steve feeling so bad because at the end of the day, he's a good guy. He loves his kids and he loved me too. Our problems—seemingly so vast and complex—boiled down to basic ignorance and a lot of misunderstanding.

Out of habit or just awkwardness, we trip over each other. Our words of apology and explanation collide. We say "if only" and "what if" and then we stop because it is clear we both think the same thing: Could we have made it as a couple? Could we still? We stop ourselves because those days are so far gone. We've made new lives. We've healed from the old wounds of our past.

We are parents together now and I think we're pretty good parents. We're finally friends again. Is that enough?

The mailman tramps up the porch steps, slaps letters into the box, and someone honks a car horn on the street. Jo and Spence laugh at something on TV.

"I hope you can forgive me, Jen," he says.

"Of course," I say. "I hope you can forgive me."

We hug each other and it's an odd embrace. We've spent so much time building barriers we don't know how to hold each other any more. Or perhaps we never did.

Steve says he needs to take a minute to himself. He says he will go around the block for a quick walk. He doesn't want the kids to see him upset.

"No problem," I say.

Steve goes through the living room and out the front door. The screen slaps back on the frame as he goes down the front steps.

THIRTY

THE KITE RIDER

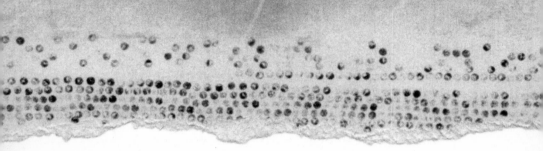

CHILDREN USED TO make me nervous, my own included. Their loud noises and screams—even in happiness—once sent me into a fit of nonsensical shaking and nail biting. I'd get rashes and feel as if my head were exploding with anxiety. Bedtime was a savior. Movie time was another blessing. The hot tub was a necessity.

I can now trace this nervous reaction to how I cried as a baby, so often and so deeply, that Janet would isolate me until I stopped or simply passed out. As a very young child, if I cried or threw a fit, I was put into cold showers or sent to sit in the corner as punishment. By the time I was four or five, I had learned to hold all feelings down and to tighten myself into a model of obedience. This was not Janet and Bud's fault. They did the best they knew how. But the result was nervousness and agitation around children and childlike behavior.

Since meeting my mother, there has been a shift in my core and children don't freak me out like they used to. Perhaps to test if it is true, I agree to go on a camp-out with my daughter's second-grade class. I am emboldened. I accept the invitation; no, I volunteer.

"But you hate school functions," Spencer says.

"Yeah, you never come to school," Jo agrees.

The three of us are in the car and they sit in the back seat. They clutch bagels with cream cheese and juice boxes, breakfast on the go.

"I do come to school," I say. I adjust the rearview to see them better. "I come to your plays. And I drive. And I've helped in the library."

"Once," Spencer says. "You did the library once."

"But I did it," I say.

Spencer chews on his bagel and with food still in his mouth, he speaks up.

"Well, I don't get it," Spencer says. "I'm the oldest. I should get you on a camp-out first."

"I'll teach a writing class for your class this year. How's that?" I suggest.

"Yeah, I guess," he says. It's as if he has missed out on something and he wears a frown under a smear of cream cheese.

Jo sticks her tongue out at her brother, as if she has won some victory.

Spencer is, of course, mortally offended. "Knock it off," he says.

Jo cannot contain herself though. She flaps her arms under her fleece rainbow poncho with the fuzzy fringe. She looks like a human butterfly.

THE REUNION CAME to a stop, four months after it began. If I went to Reno, and I did three times, the visits went well. Being in my mother's presence infused me with a peace and calm and love. The trouble came when we were apart. My mind, with stories of abandonment, fear, despair, loneliness, anger, and sorrow, would overcome me. And Catherine couldn't keep up. She couldn't call, check in, or come to Portland. The logistics were too much. She said she felt backed into a corner and trapped. She felt I was too needy.

I thought that once I found my mother, I would instantly be over all my old wounds, but it doesn't work like that. My adoption had shredded us both. In equal part, we each had much more healing to do, and for me it was time to go it alone for a while.

MY KIDS DID meet the family. Jo discovered a new cousin and Spencer had fun playing with Jessie and her little boy.

When we left Reno, Spencer said, "They look like you, Mom, but they are nothing like you, you know?"

With anyone else, I might have asked questions but with Spencer—I understood.

THE CHAPERONES CLUSTER in the gymnasium, which is thick with the smells of rubber balls and dirty socks. I wear a nametag around my neck that reads: *Josephine's Mom*. Jo presents me with the files of the two children who are to ride with me. They are Sarin and Ray.

"Already I have a problem," I say. "You are not on my list."

All four feet of Jo Jo stands up taller, paisley poncho draped around her body, her hood on her head.

"Mo-om," she says. "We talked about this. You have to drive other kids. It's the rule."

I push her hood back and stomp my foot.

"I don't get this rule. I want to be with you," I insist.

"Mom," she says. She pulls her hood back up and stomps her foot right back at me. "This is class time. I have to be independent."

It's all a show. I already know I am not to have Jo in my car. Her teacher has made it clear that I am to allow Jo her own "self-sufficient outdoor experience," without my preferential treatment. While I'm with the group, I am everyone's mommy. This way, the other children, whose mothers could not come, do not feel left out.

I take this as a reminder of a lesson I know all too well. The wrong kind of mothering and even overmothering can be as bad as no mothering. The act of nurturing requires such delicate balance. I know. I know.

"Fine," I say, pouting. "Be independent. Show me how it's done."

Jo flits away, grinning over her shoulder, and I join the group of waiting parents.

WHAT DO I think of the life I have lived?

I once had so many regrets, wishing for less abuse and more expedient understanding of circumstances but these feelings no longer hold me hostage.

My life has been my life and I have learned the best I knew how.

I've tried as hard as any human could have. Now I've met Catherine, I feel a new self mature within my core and my old sad and protective self is being shed like the skin of a snake. I'm working myself free. I'm emerging into a new world.

My view widens to the point where I can forgive the people from my past—Richard, Peggy, Deb, her kids, Bryan, Bud, Janet, Auntie Carol. What's done is done. I can also see my own part in our mutual story. I can see the tricks my mind played on me. I can see how I even attracted so much negativity and hardship. I have learned the power of a traumatized mind.

I also now have the luxury, space, and inner peace to be philosophical about the past. I feel I have learned so much; I have grown as a human being in this human family. And I get to ponder how the suffering we go through has the potential to make us more vivid and alive. I remind myself of the pressure a rock must go through to become a crystal. I have experienced that pressure myself. I feel refined.

Most of all, I am grateful for my life and to Catherine for allowing time together to fulfill the biological need. I needed to get fully born into this life and my mother overcame her shame and her desire for secrecy to give that to me. What more could I want?

IN THE CENTER of the gym, the children of the class are assembled in a circle. They are short, tall, skinny, thick, short-haired, long-haired, blond, brunette, black hair, and nearly every race. Their teacher, a high-spirited woman with boundless stores of positive energy, gives them last-minute instructions.

This is a school designed around the method of Maria Montessori. The prime objective is to follow the child. Adults are guides, not teachers. Children explore the world and lead their own learning process. Each stage of development is considered.

Jo pays close attention and is so earnest as her beloved teacher speaks. She stands tall, her shoulders back and her chin high, poised at the age of independence. She now knows who she is. She is, very much, her own person.

IT IS COMMON for an adoptee to search for her father's people when the reunion with the birth mother simmers down. I am no exception. I did search.

This is when I learned of the impossible birthday, September 19, 1945. I also learned that Bill Wright died in the year 2005. He had cancer.

While he lived, Bill had been fruitful.

I found three more brothers—Tom, John, and David—as well as a sister named Sarah. I've met them all save Tom, and found my siblings to be quiet, contemplative, and sweet people with a kind of vulnerability and depth I didn't experience in Catherine's presence. She must have been the sunny side of the match and Bill was the dark side. I find I am surprisingly comfortable with my father's children. They have been welcoming, polite, understanding, and genuine. I like them.

I am told Bill had four wives and loved them all.

Bill served in Vietnam and was honorably discharged.

Bill was a Christian man who read the Bible nearly every day. He used to go around his house writing scriptures, as well as his own thoughts, on legal pads.

Bill settled in a town very near Winlock called Yelm. He had a hobby of digging in the dirt of his yard where he would unearth rocks to make walking paths and stone walls. He made the soil of his garden supple and soft enough to grow a bountiful garden of strawberries and vegetables. He cooked for his family—in fact, my sister Sarah tells me it was Bill's cooking that brought the many wives and children together. They all loved his food.

Bill had a dark side, flashbacks from Vietnam. Another ghost that haunted him was his own childhood. His mother, named Georgia, abandoned him as a little boy. His grandmother raised him. His mother, who drank, came and went. Bill never knew his own father. It's suspected Georgia was a prostitute.

During his worst attacks, Bill would leave his family and go off by himself for days, sometimes weeks, to wrestle deep depression.

Sarah told me Bill, when lucid, had been a good man and a good father. "Family was important to him," she told me. She said her father had been generous and kind. He loved his kids. Even at his worst, he never harmed his own.

When he died, he wrote all his recipes down and left them to his youngest son, David.

"OKAY NOW," THE guide says, clapping her hands. "Find your chaperone and let's grab our gear."

I am on the lookout for my charges, Sarin and Ray, and they are quick to appear in front of me with little nametags around their necks. Both children have impossibly dark eyes and tentative smiles. Sarin has long dark hair in pigtails. Ray has a crew cut. Sarin is clearly of Eastern Indian descent and Ray is of Asian descent. I wonder if they are adopted children but don't make that assumption. This is an international school, after all.

Sarin and Ray are weighted down with sleeping bags and backpacks. They shift their bundles in their arms. "Can I help?" I offer.

They both shake their heads in the same way at the same time. Their expressions are quite serious for ones so young.

"Right," I say. "You are supposed to do it yourselves."

They nod, so earnest.

"Okay," I say. "Let's go."

We weave out of the gym. Jo is in another group. I sneak a wave in her direction but she pretends to ignore me.

WE FORM A caravan of cars, vans, and trucks and everyone follows the guide in the lead. We have cell phones and maps and a three-hour drive to complete. Our route is through a maze of freeways, down to the ocean, and up to the edge of the state. The teaching is about Lewis and Clark, that team of explorers who ended their trek across the U.S. just outside Astoria, Oregon.

Once underway, I announce that I have a book on tape.

"Okay," Sarin agrees.

"Sure," says Ray.

I am surprised by their agreeability. Jo and Spencer would never consent with such speed.

"Do you want to know what it's about?" I ask.

They don't really seem to care but I go ahead and explain how the story is about a little boy in China who is tied to a kite against his will and sent to the heavens to test the wind. It's titled *The Kite Rider.*

"If you hate it, we'll do music or something else," I say as I put in the first CD.

"Okay," Ray says. Sarin says nothing. She looks out the window.

They are so well mannered and polite—nothing like the flapping poncho and the sulking of an hour ago. I look from child to child and they are so very familiar to me. International school or not, these kids are adopted.

Later, the guide will confirm that Sarin is from India and Ray is from Vietnam. I will be told of struggles that plague them—the lack of trust, the need for structure and routine, learning challenges, deep fears, tender open hearts, and an eagerness to please.

The CD book begins with the sound of gongs and the deep voice of the narrator. All three of us are taken in right away when the boy is orphaned in the first chapter.

IF I LET myself imagine being Tara Wright rather than Jennifer Lauck, I have to ask not what would have become of me, but instead, what would I have missed? Would I have become an investigative reporter and then a writer? Would I have slept in a tent in the Rocky Mountains, under a rainbow-ringed moon? Would I have hiked dusty roads, asking myself about the nature of my mind? Would I have sat in front of an enlightened master and heard him speak Tibetan, while giving me a thumbs up? Would I have done one prostration, let alone one hundred thousand for the benefit of all beings? Would I have met Tylanni, Rinpoche, or Anne? Would I have loved, fought, and made babies with Steve? Would there be Jo? Would there be Spencer? Would I have found the love of Rogelio? Would there be me, as I am now, a middle-aged woman ripening into an old woman with such a tale to tell?

I suppose it's not about being Jennifer Lauck or Tara Wright, it's about what I will now do with my life. I must continue to ask myself deep questions about what has come to pass, which include these: *Did I learn? Did I grow? Can I say I am a woman—no matter my name—who brings healing and love? Or will I forever be defined and governed by what I have lost? What is the value of what has passed?*

Big questions.

We shall see.

JUST THE OTHER day, Roger looked up my name in Chinese (which is just like him since he's a scholar of ancient Chinese medicine). He said Jennifer translates to be Zhen Ni Fa and this means—among many things—green jade woman. Of course, a green jade woman is Tara.

I will remain as Jennifer Caste Lauck for this life. That is who I am and who I always was. But I suppose I am also Tara. I am Jampel Sherab too. And I'm none of these. I find myself, these days, beyond explanation.

Such a state can be a great relief.

THE CLASS IS to visit a Lewis and Clark museum and I turn off the CD and pull over for the first stop of the day.

"You know, this is a pretty scary book," I say. "Are you guys okay with it?"

"No, it's not," Sarin says. "It's really good."

"We get to listen again when we get back in, right?" Ray asks.

They lean forward, stretching the seat belt straps to the limits. Adopted children like to know what's going to happen next. They want continuity and a sense of control. I see these desires in their faces and hear them in their questions.

"Yes," I say, "of course."

We pile out of the car and I act as vigilant guide, making sure they have lunches, coats, and their note pads. I get them to the curb safely. I rest my hands on their shoulders—the lightest of touch, just enough, not too much. Adopted children don't like to be smothered. But they will smother you, if they let you get close enough.

Sarin and Ray ease close to me. They lean into my sides, barely touching beyond a confirmation of contact.

As we cross the road together, I feel a rise of surprising love for these two children—it's as big as what I feel for Jo and Spencer. All this time, I have kept myself so isolated from the world and I have been so full of fear that I did not think it possible to open my heart to strangers, but look. Love is here.

IT'S NOT TRUE that I didn't have any identity. The problem was that I had too many identities—all of them flimsy at best. My Self, prior to meeting Catherine, was a patchwork quilt, a jagged mosaic of trial and error. I am now in a phase of refinement.

I was a writer and that is who I remain.

I was a mother and that is who I am too.

I was a Buddhist and now remain a curious student, although I am now more like an Ekhart Tolle-yogini-Buddha-Daoist. I also dig Byron Katie, I think Jesus rocks, and I'm pretty sure John Lennon was enlightened. I'd make a bet on it.

Before I met Catherine, I played piano for years, studying classical music. I bought a tabla and took lessons from a small Indian man. I also had a small accordion-style instrument, from India as well, and I was trying to figure that machine out. I even took voice lessons. I was trying to find myself through the mastery of music. I have given all that up. I am not a musician (although I love music).

Before I met Catherine, I studied dance, a high-test form of ballet, for twenty years. I stood on tiptoes, did deep pliés and attempted running leaps. I made achingly slow progress. I was trying to find myself through the mastery of dance. I have given that up too. I am not a dancer (although I love to dance).

Before I met Catherine, I became a Tibetan Buddhist, meditated, considered becoming a nun and—well, you know that story. I was trying to find myself through the mastery of spirit. I am not a Tibetan. I don't have time to meditate hours of each day away and I certainly am not a monastic. I do my Tara meditation nearly every day. Tara is enough for me.

I am now a person who prefers chocolate ice cream.

My favorite food is Japanese.

I don't like cake.

I do like pastries.

My favorite tree is the red oak in my back yard.

My favorite flower is the rose.

My favorite color is brown, a deep, rich, earthy shade of sable brown.

AFTER LUNCH, THE children collectively play on and around the picnic tables. They chase each other and make games of tag and hide and seek.

Sarin remains outside the group. She holds her journal to her chest. Her ponytails have come undone and she has the elastics on her wrist for safekeeping. Ray is off on the other side of the group, sitting at a bench in solitude.

The other chaperones are all together, at the tables too, and they chat as they eat.

I sit at a bench, on my own and within earshot of Sarin.

"Do you want me to fix your hair?" I ask.

I am pretty sure Sarin will say no to my offer but she smiles and nods. She wriggles the bands off her wrist and hands them to me.

I comb her hair with my fingers and it slides over my skin, so dark that it shines. It's thick too. "You have the prettiest hair," I tell her. "I love it."

She says thank you, very polite.

I put the elastics into place, careful not to pull or tug.

"Is that good?" I ask.

She nods and sits down next to me on the bench.

It doesn't bother me that she sits here with me, so quiet. If she were Jo, I'd worry that she didn't feel well or was unhappy. Jo isn't the kind of child to sit on a bench, apart from the crowd. Spencer isn't either. But I was, and so is Sarin.

At my feet is a basket of yarn I travel with. I knit from a skein of gray wool that feeds out of the basket—back and forth I go—creating something from nothing.

"What are you making?" Sarin asks.

"Oh, just a scarf," I say.

Sarin plays with the yarn that feeds into my needles and we say no more.

Knitting isn't about the scarf but is about soothing anxiety. A therapist I know also said knitting can help reform the trauma structures built into my brain. It has something to do with using both hands, crossing the axis and repetitive motion but I don't really understand the science. I just know knitting helps calm me down. If knitting can also help realign my brain—pass the yarn.

"I knit too," Sarin says.

"You do?"

She nods, big dark eyes of melted chocolate.

"Finger knitting, most of the time," she adds. "I like it though. It makes me feel better."

"I hear you, little sister," I say. "You want some yarn?"

She smiles when I call her little sister, just a trace of a smile but declines my offer. Finally, she gets off the bench and says she's going to fill her water bottle before we go.

As she walks over to the fountain, Ray comes to where I sit and plunks down on the bench. "Whatcha making?" he asks.

THIS IS THE story I tell myself about Catherine.

She is a product of her environment—of her land. She lives where gambling, prostitution, and speedy marriages and divorces are the norm. Her cells have been rearranged by the many nuclear bomb blasts that have occurred just a few hundred miles south. Radioactive winds have blown over her roof and have been inhaled and exhaled a trillion times. Her state contains a national sacrifice zone—the only one I know of in the U.S.—where a wide swath of land is uninhabitable and will be for countless generations.

Catherine also happens to be one of an estimated 1.5 million American girls who were forced to sacrifice their babies under Nazi-like conditions of terror and fear. The stories of women strapped down during labor, of having babies mercilessly wrenched away, and of being forced to sign documents that were not legal are enough to make even me, a hardened journalist, revolted.

My mother, like so many others, was shunned and shamed and forced to be silent for the whole of her life. Many girls never went on to have more children. Many more have died alone with their sorrow. Too many have not searched for their children.

What happens inside a person under such conditions? What slips inside the brain or the psyche or even the soul to make such an experience bearable? How does a person—a mother—go on? I cannot know the answer to these questions. They are impossible for me to ponder.

My heart breaks for my mother and what she has endured. I have no right to judge her and when I find I am judging her, I make myself think again—I push my heart to open wider still. I look for the love that is my original connection to Catherine and I keep my focus there.

I wish my mother well.

BACK IN THE car for the last leg of our drive, the children are eager to pick up the story of the kite rider, who now ties himself to a kite and has become the one who casts himself out—despite the danger.

Sarin and Ray are very quiet. They eat snacks. They pay sharp attention.

This is no Disney tale. In fact, it's a terrible tale of cruelty to children and the abuses of those who hold power. The plot twists like paper in the wind. The powerful get more powerful. The weak become weaker. In the end, the child nearly dies and finally goes blind in one eye. He cannot continue as a kite rider. Instead he makes kites and decides a better life is one where he keeps his feet firmly on the ground.

I like the book, I guess. It's an award winner recommended by the librarian but I hope it wasn't too much. I turn off the CD.

"Whew," I say. "What a story." I practically wipe my brow.

Sarin and Ray say nothing. Neither of them breathes a sigh of relief.

If Spencer and Jo were in the car, they would be outraged, surprised, and even shocked at the injustices in the story and the way the characters behaved. Both would ask a thousand questions that I'd attempt to answer while also trying to protect them from the fact that outrageous injustice exists.

But for Sarin and Ray, the story of a child cast on the winds is not unusual. A child who suffers isn't something new. They are old beyond being seven and nine.

As I watch them in the rearview mirror, these little recognizable strangers who occupy my heart, I wonder how far they will be unfurled in their own lives, before, like me, they find a way to reel themselves in again. Will they go home to their mothers and families in India and Vietnam? Will their adoptive families have the courage and wisdom to give them that gift, even if the children don't ask to go home? Will those families also be there to support their charges if birth families reject them a second time around? Will they survive? Will they be happy? Will they be whole?

We cross a long bridge that takes us to the edge of North America, just outside Astoria. Tonight the class will camp at a park a few miles beyond Fort Clatsop, where Lewis and Clark stopped their westward journey, took a break for the wet winter, and then turned around to return east. This bridge, more than two miles long, crosses the Columbia River as the river meets the Pacific Ocean. The children look over the waves of the sea. Do they know, not far away, lies Russia and beyond is Vietnam and India?

Sarin asks if she can open the window. She wants to feel the wind on her face.

"You bet," I say. I roll down all the western windows and the inside of the car fills with the salty taste of the sea. Wind whips napkins and empty wrappers around the interior of the car. Sarin and Ray laugh.

The purity of their sound rearranges my cells and brings such hope to my heart and soul.

ON THE OTHER end of the bridge, the caravan reaches its destination and we all park.

In tight clusters, children emerge from cars and run to the campground, chasing each other and yelling to unleash pent-up energy. Jo Jo sprints off with her best friends, Grace and Marbella. Their giggles fly through the air.

The other drivers look tired, worn out, and even harried.

I get out of the car and stretch my arms and my legs. Sarin and Ray do the same. I am not tired.

"Good trip, you guys," I say. "You are wonderful travelers."

"Do we go back home with you?" Ray asks, taking hold of my right hand.

"Yes, of course, I'm your guide."

Sarin takes my left hand. "Good," she says.

Before we cross the road and join the others, I look both ways, which is rather silly and redundant. There's no car on the road and we are the only ones out here. But I can't help it.

Off in the distance is the ocean and the sun goes down, turning the sea the color of steel. I get Sarin and Ray across the road, safe and sound, and release them to the group.

The End

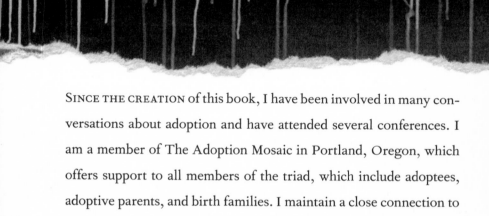

SINCE THE CREATION of this book, I have been involved in many conversations about adoption and have attended several conferences. I am a member of The Adoption Mosaic in Portland, Oregon, which offers support to all members of the triad, which include adoptees, adoptive parents, and birth families. I maintain a close connection to the leaders in the field and am a member of Concerned United Birthparents as well as the American Adoption Congress.

My general feeling about adoption is that we are not thinking very well about this very important subject, nor are we applying common sense to the biological connection of mother and child.

Is this lack of thought due to the fact that there is just so much money to be made in the field of adoption? From lawyers to agencies to intermediaries and over to churches, adoption is a big business.

Perhaps our lack of thought also comes from a strong need to idealize family and to behave as if everything is perfect—when it's not.

It's hard to know why we do as we do, but when we adopt, we face a myriad of complex challenges and opportunities that must be faced, discussed, and resolved.

Adoptive parents must be better informed.

Birth mothers must be better informed.

Adoptees must be better informed.

IT IS DISTRESSING to learn that the U.S. leads the world as the single largest adoption nation. It seems startling to me that Americans are so fast on the scene of international disasters, and we scoop up orphan children and have them adopted into U.S. homes before body counts are added up.

Imagine if a collective of Chinese emissaries rushed to our shores after a disaster like Hurricane Katrina and took off with Louisiana babies. Or say a collective of Australian humanitarians came to Manhattan after 9/11 and hauled away orphans. These scenarios are ludicrous, and yet this is what American representatives are doing under the guise of being helpful.

Helpful is keeping children within their own culture and empowering the people of those lands with resources, food, medicine, and water. Helpful is helping children to grieve and move forward in their lives with dignity. It is not helpful to take a child, in the midst of a crisis, from her land and her people.

Nor is it helpful, within our boundaries, to take a child from a mother due to her economic struggles, her age, or even her education. It is helpful to offer support, education, and solutions.

We can fund wars and build bombs, but we cannot empower mothers to keep and care for their children?

Yes, much thought and much conversation are needed on adoption.

The high instances of mental health disturbance in adoptive children and grown adoptees are stunning, and yet, there is little to no recognition of why. I once listened to a high-level government official and lawyer (who is an adoptive mother as well) explain that she felt there were higher instances of mental health issues in adoptees due to poor reporting—prior to placement—by birth parents.

Her comments held no recognition of the practical and well-documented evidence that shows trauma occurs in a baby at the time of separation from the birth mother.

This gap in the conversation needs to be straddled and I hope we, in future generations, can recognize that displaced children have legacies, genetics, and lineages that predate placement in their adoptive homes.

Think of this practically. If you or I found a small child in the aisles of a grocery store—lost and crying for her mother—would we snap the child up, strap her into our car, and drive away while admonishing her to "forget that mommy, I'm your mommy now"? Of course not. That would be kidnapping. Yet this is exactly what we do when we adopt and somehow this is legal.

Adoption, in an open situation, is humane.

Adoption where the baby is given a time of physical proximity to the birth mother is also more enlightened as it allows a more healthy development of the child's brain.

Reunion, at some point in the adoptee life, is vital.

I do not have answers for how to structure adoption to make these scenarios manageable.

I do believe women, especially the educated women of the West, have the power to heal this world. I also believe that in honoring and empowering women worldwide, we will certainly come to the obvious conclusion that our future is our children. To create generations of children nurtured by their mother's touch and care will make this a world worth living in.

I suggest more conversation, more compassion, much more common sense, and much better thinking. I also suggest we place children not last but first.

EIGHTEEN MONTHS AFTER we took a break from the reunion, Catherine and I spoke again and reinitiated our reunion process. In our time apart, we had both entered support groups and have now agreed to know each other with care and caution. We may never find our way fully home to each other. Perhaps sometimes, it's enough to just try.

ACKNOWLEDGMENTS

WRITING IS A MOST personal journey, but to bring a book to the world is a collective endeavor. This story may not have been written, and certainly would not have been published, had it not been for the conviction, insight, and perseverance of my agent, Anne Edelstein. Thank you, Anne, for your high standards in craft and storytelling. Thank you for telling me, again and again, what this story was truly about.

Thank you to Seal Press and my editor Brooke Warner. It is an honor to work with fearless women who are ready to take on the tough issues of our time.

Thank you to Nancy Verrier. I am quite certain no one else could have pressed me to take that final step in the journey and to finally find my mother.

Thank you Rogelio, the kids, and of course, Steve. It's not easy to live with a writer or to understand her ways. My family bends around me and I am blessed.

Thank you to my beloved friend Anne Gudger for listening to each revision with such interest and insight.

Thank you to my mentor, Dinah Lenney, and to the Rainier Writing Workshop as well as Stan Rubin and Judith Kitchen.

And great enduring thanks to my spiritual teachers: H.H., Rinpoche, Jetsuma, Anne Klein of Dawn Mountain, and Joanna Macy.

© STACY VRIESE

ABOUT THE AUTHOR

JENNIFER LAUCK HAS WRITTEN THREE MEMOIRS and a collection of essays, including the *New York Times* bestselling *Blackbird: A Childhood Lost and Found*. She has her MFA in creative writing from Pacific Lutheran University, her BA in journalism from Montana State, and was an award winning investigative TV reporter.

Lauck has studied Tibetan Buddhism for nearly ten years, is a dedicated meditation student, and has received teachings from many great masters including the H.H. Dalai Lama, Lama Adzom Rinpoche, and Eco-philosopher Joanna Macy.

Lauck teaches writing in area high schools for Literary Arts, conducts private seminars on her technique known as Transformative Writing, and speaks nationally on issues of adoption, motherhood, transcendence, happiness, and writing as a way to heal. She is at work on a novel and makes her home in Portland, Oregon, where she is happily married and raising her son, Spencer and her daughter, Josephine.

Learn more about Lauck, her teachings, and her writing at www.jenniferlauck.com.